AN AUTOBIOGRAPHY OF
AN UNKNOWN WRITER

RON'S PREVIOUS EFFORTS
The Good, the Bad, and the Unpublishable

BOOKS

- *Working and Managing in a New Age,* published in hardcover and then mass paperback by Ivy Books, a division of Random House, also available in Spanish and Portuguese, Ron's best-selling book
- *Humanity Sucks: Zen and the Art of Transhuman Evolution, or Charles Darwin Meets the Buddha at Woodstock,* Ron's favorite of all his books, available at Amazon.com
- *Sexual Harassment Can Be Deadly,* available at Amazon.com
- *Twelve Reasons Why No Decent, Intelligent Person Can Be a Christian Fundamentalist,* available at Amazon.com, published under the name Sedgewick Patton
- *Making Work Fun: Doing Business With a Sense of Humor,* published by Shamrock Press, limited availability on eBay and in used bookstores
- *Zen Sensualism,* published under the name Dale Watts
- *A Romantic's Guide to San Francisco,* published under the name Dale Watts
- *Reading to Write: 50 Books Every Aspiring Writer Should Read*
- *Reading to Think: A Thought-Provoking Guide to Over 100 of the World's Most Thought-Provoking Books*

- *Slightly to the Left of St. Louis: A Guide for the Progressive Newcomer*
- *The Joys of Unitarian Universalism: Religion for People Who Think*
- *Murder at the Nudist Club: A Revealing Mystery*
- *Negotiating with Fanatics: What to Do When Win/Win Won't Work*

COMPLETED MANUSCRIPTS THAT WERE NEVER PUBLISHED

- The Dark Side of the Moon
- Affirmative Re-Action
- The Truly Enlightened Don't Write Books
- Would You Like to Be a Character in My Next Novel?
- Writers, Lovers, and Other Fools
- Life is Uncertain, Eat Dessert First
- The Scream

MANUSCRIPTS UNLIKELY TO EVER BE COMPLETED

- The Last Silly Love Song
- Who Is Killing the Great Lovers of San Francisco?

A LIMITED LIST OF PUBLISHED STORIES AND ARTICLES

- "Random Acts of Good and Evil," *PanGaia* 37 (2003)
- "A Gathering of Eagles," *PanGaia* 43 (2006)
- "Time to Get Tough on Employee Performance," *Federal Times* (December 3, 2001)
- "Reforming the Federal Labor Relations System," *Federal Labor Relations Reporter* (May 1989)
- "Why Albuquerque?" *Prime Time* (November 2003)
- "Screw the South," *Liberal Opinions* (December 2003)
- And many more too horrible to mention

PRAISE FOR RON'S PREVIOUS BOOKS

*Making Work Fun:
Doing Business with a Sense of Humor*

"I think this book will do very, very well. It's right on the money."

—Ken Blanchard,
The One Minute Manager

*Humanity Sucks: Zen and the Art of
Transhuman Evolution, or Charles Darwin
Meets the Buddha at Woodstock*

"Sex, drugs, & Rock 'n' Roll, plus Buddha, Darwin, jokes, cartoons, videos, and movies. It's a sometimes confusing mix, but always interesting and guaranteed to challenge all your ideas about the purpose of human life."

—Paula Edward-Presson,
Amazon.com

Working and Managing in a New Age

"This is a slim volume that is packed with pearls of wisdom…This book is a jewel that I would recommend highly as an addition to everyone's library."

—Jean Spector,
Human Resource Development Review

"Garland's discussion presents new ideals of management and work which offers positive guidelines for personal company assessment and tools for transforming the art of management."

—Midwest Book Review

"Deftly contrasts the old age values that may still be lurking within your organization with New Age concepts you may be struggling to implement."

—Body, Mind, & Spirit Magazine

An
AUTOBIOGRAPHY
of an
UNKNOWN
WRITER

*From Cowboy Stories through the
Sexual Revolution to Beyond Humanity*

RON GARLAND

LUMINARE PRESS
WWW.LUMINAREPRESS.COM

An Autobiography of an Unknown Writer: From Cowboy Stories through
the Sexual Revolution to Beyond Humanity
Copyright © 2021 by Ron Garland

All rights reserved. This book or any portion thereof may not be reproduced
or used in any manner whatsoever without the express written permission of
the publisher, except for the use of brief quotations in a book review.

Printed in the United States of America

Luminare Press
442 Charnelton St.
Eugene, OR 97401
www.luminarepress.com

LCCN: 2021914793
ISBN: 978-1-64388-733-3

Dedication

To all the unknown writers who desire to create a better world through the power of their words and who persist against great odds.

Table of Contents

Writing Is a Dangerous Profession 1

A Compulsion to Write 11

A Writer's Point of View, or My First Tragedy 16

Another Embarrassing Failure 23

Discovering Female and
African American Authors (1963) 28

Becoming a Sportswriter 35

The 1960s: Sex, Drugs, and Radical
Student Newspapers 41

Mapping New York State 45

California in the 1970s 51

The Heartbreak Manuscript 64

Small Successes, a Big Decision 70

Life with Baby Shakes Things Up 76

The St. Louis Blues 86

The E-Book Era 93

The Power of Anger 106

Blah, Blah, Blogs 112

Things Fall Apart, the Sinner Cannot Hold 119

We Get Lucky in Vegas	126
Fear and Loathing in Las Vegas (2016)	130
Do You Remember Your Life in Chronological Order?	134
Thoughts and Prayers	162
Conversation with My Agent	200
Why I Am Not a Survivalist	206
The Last Chapter	209
Another Chapter, or a Somewhat Happier Ending	212
Acknowledgments	221
Want to Contact the Author?	223

POT-SHOTS NO. 3273

MORE BOOKS HAVE RESULTED FROM SOMEBODY'S NEED TO WRITE THAN FROM ANYBODY'S NEED TO READ.

© ASHLEIGH BRILLIANT 1985.

"The writer is, first, genetically predisposed to write."
—Jayne Anne Phillips, "Why She Writes"

"As writers, we know what the 'writer's high' feels like, the sense of elation we feel when we're cooking away on a project. The world and all of its problems melt away. Our lives have purpose, direction, meaning."
—Jack Heffron, *The Writer's Idea Book*

"Remember, it is possible to have a perfectly happy and balanced life without ever writing a book, short story, or even a poem. You can take up less dangerous pursuits such as snowboarding or sky diving, instead…If you are a true writer, you will find what I just said laughable. Because for you, writing is a way of surviving in the world, the medium through which you make sense of your life. Besides, you can't think of a more fun way to spend your time."
—Thrity Umrigar, *The Space Between Us*

"A man's true delight is to do the things he was made for."
—Marcus Aurelius, *Meditations*

MUSICAL PRELUDE:
"Paperback Writer," The Beatles
"Every Fool Has a Rainbow," Merle Haggard

CHAPTER 1

Writing Is a Dangerous Profession

I've been writing and selling books and stories for seven decades, and still few people know who I am. It's time for one final story before I die. It's time to tell the story I know best—my own. I started writing stories when I was four. My first muse was murdered when I was five. I sold my first story when I was in the third grade and thought I was on my way to a great career as a writer. By the fourth grade, I was suspended from school for one of my controversial articles. Such are the joys and agonies of the writing life.

I was born to be a writer. It was in my genes. Unfortunately, it wasn't in my genes to be a great writer or a famous writer. I've written more than twenty book-length manuscripts, but only twelve of those have been published, and none of them were best sellers or won any major awards. You will not find my name in the Writers Hall of Fame, and I won't be buried in Poets' Corner. I'm more likely to be buried in the Tomb of the Unknown Writer. Actually, I don't want to be buried at all. Just lay me on a huge pile of my unsold books and cremate me.

My mother was an elementary school teacher during World War II, and she taught me to read when I was only three. I was writing my own little stories soon thereafter and started selling them when I was eight.

I wrote cowboy stories and sold them to my friends and classmates. My third grade teacher thought it was cute and showed me how to use a mimeograph machine so I could make multiple copies of the story and get mass distribution. Well, I could sell five to ten copies of each story for two cents a copy. Keep in mind, in those days, 1956, I could buy a small carton of chocolate milk for two cents in the school cafeteria. This was serious cash.

I was hooked on writing forever. *What a great way to make money*, I thought. *I make up little stories, and my classmates give me pennies.*

However, writing is a dangerous profession, even in grade school. In the third grade, I stuck with what I knew: cowboy stories. Not that I was much of a cowboy myself. I did have a pony, and I could ride and jump short fences with my horse, Silver, but my basic knowledge of the cowboy genre came from watching *The Lone Ranger, Roy Rogers, Hopalong Cassidy,* and the like.

When I decided to branch out to a new field of writing, it was a disaster. They say "write what you know," and it turns out this cliché is good advice. (How does something get to be a cliché? Lots of people say it over and over, and it contains some element of truth.) In fourth grade, my classmates urged me to expand my talents beyond cowboy stories. To be precise, they wanted me to write a story about how babies are made, as this was a mystery in which they all had a great interest.

I agreed to give my public what it wanted. Unfortunately, I didn't have a clue as to how babies were made. I was outside of the "write what you know" guidance, but I plowed ahead and didn't let my ignorance stand in the way. I was a successful writer, the best-selling writer in my fourth grade class. I was creative. I could make up cowboy stories, so why not make this up too? So I did.

My story (I suppose you could say this was my first attempt at science fiction) had almost every fact wrong except that the baby did somehow come out of a woman's body. I called this portal to the human world the woman's "lower stomach," because I didn't have an inkling about female anatomy, had never heard the words vagina or uterus, and didn't have internet access or even an unabridged dictionary, to do any meaningful research. The story had the creative title of "Babies and Storks: Truth or Myth." I was way beyond the stork theory. After all, the 1950s were the height of the baby boom, and you didn't need to be a gynecologist to see that there were women everywhere with large stomachs immediately before the arrival of a new baby. I had figured out that much but not much more.

Despite my total stupidity, my public loved the story, and I sold an all-time record of fourteen copies. After I realized what a hot product I had, I raised the price to a nickel after the first eight copies sold. I was a dirty little capitalist.

Unfortunately, the critics didn't care for the story—the critics being the teachers, the principal, and the superintendent of schools. I was sent to the principal's office, where I was interrogated at length about my sources. Thank god Mr. Conrad didn't know about waterboarding, or I would have died, since I had no sources to divulge, and for whatever reason, he refused to believe that I had made the whole thing up, although it was the only logical explanation since the story was so factually inaccurate.

The principal seemed certain there was a conspiracy here and that my older cousins, Billy and Donnie, had put me up to this and given me lots of half-truths about the baby-making process. They hadn't. The story was pure fiction. After a couple hours, he accepted that either my confession of being the lone writer was true or that I was not going to crack and give up my sources.

The principal insisted that I write a retraction, coupled with an apology, and give a copy to each person who had foolishly bought a copy of the story. Just to rub salt into my wound (and I was wounded, in a state of great fear and anxiety, as I had no notion as to what exactly I had done wrong or why it was so shockingly wrong to all the adults), the principal insisted I return all my ill-gotten pennies and nickels.

I wrote my first retraction and returned all the money, but this was just the beginning of my troubles, embarrassments, and problems. I was suspended for two days. My parents were called, and I got more questions and lectures from them that night when I got home. No one had explained the "facts of life" to me. It was clear I had written something profane and vulgar and stumbled into a topic that was so forbidden that the adults could not tell even me why it was forbidden. I was terrified for days that if I should suddenly and prematurely die for some reason—like acute embarrassment—I would go directly to hell for having authored such a horrible tale.

The principal took away my mimeograph privileges and told me to stop writing any stories whatsoever. I had no problem with this at the time as I was still in a state of shock and afraid to write anything new. My first case of writers' block—or writers' shock.

My classmates split into two groups. One group deserted me, having been told (by certain teachers and their own parents, I assume) that I was a dangerous person who might lead them into a life of crime, drug abuse, and debauchery (none of us had any clue as to what drug abuse was, much less debauchery). The second group saw me as a rebel who had challenged the status quo, the establishment, the adult world that possessed exciting and secret information that they were determined to keep from us. I called the first group by the imaginative label of "the scaredy cats," and the second group I called "true friends." This second group encouraged me to write in secret and help them find out the truth about baby making.

This is how I came to understand that to write something, a writer first often needed to do a little research. I started my quest by going to the high school library and trying to do find some answers. I was able to make a tiny amount of progress. I learned that making babies involved sex, but there was nothing in the library that explained exactly what sex was. This was my first experience with circuitous definitions. Sex was defined as intercourse, intercourse as coitus, coitus as sex, ad nauseam, but there was never a real explanation of any of these terms.

Next, I tried the public library and found a little more information. There were a handful of medical books and books on human anatomy that allowed me to start to piece the facts together. There wasn't anything along the lines of *The Joy of Sex* in those ancient days.

So I had to learn all the details of sexual interaction from porn. It wasn't easy to get porn when you were ten years old. In 1958, in Middle America, it probably wasn't easy to get porn if you were seventy years old.

I found one bookstore in nearby Cape Girardeau, Missouri (the hometown of right-wing hatemonger Rush Limbaugh, who was a jerk even as a kid). The bookstore had a little back room with "adult" books. I slipped in, glanced at a few, and wanted to take them all home with me. Upon a quick and secretive reading in the back room, with one eye out for the clerk to make sure I didn't get caught, I still didn't grasp the full significance of sexual intercourse, but I picked up enough to know that I wanted to know more, and these books seemed to be the only available source of such information.

I wasn't a complete dummy. I knew the clerk would never sell me even one such book. However, I was clever and devious. I went out into the street and found some weirdo who looked like he would do anything for a little money to buy beer or cigarettes and asked him to go into the bookstore, seek out the back room, and buy me a book. I would give him some extra money for his trouble. Amazingly, he agreed. I told him to buy a book called *Southern Sluts*, because it had a nice cover of an attractive blonde walking on a Florida beach wearing only the bottom part of a bathing suit. The picture was slightly from the back, so you didn't see her breasts. She was looking back over her shoulder at two guys who had gigantic smiles on their faces like they had just won a million bucks.

The bookstore transaction went off without a hitch, and the weirdo (John) and I established a positive working relationship that I used often in the years ahead to obtain everything from actual porn to more literary sex stories, such as *Lady Chatterley's Lover*, and pop porn or soft smut such as *Peyton Place*.

My relationship with John taught me an important lesson. Every human being, no matter how stupid, ignorant, or apparently despicable, is good for something. Another writers' cliché is that everyone you meet is grist for the mill. In other words, every person, no matter how humble, can teach a writer something, and John taught me a lot, even if indirectly, by purchasing porn.

Ironically, the money for the adult books came from my job mowing the grass at the Methodist/Lutheran churches' cemetery. The churches probably would not have been happy to learn that money was circulating from their collection plates to an adult store.

I had to read *Southern Sluts* several times to fully understand it all. I kept getting sexually aroused, which was annoying, since I had not hit puberty. I could get an erection but couldn't ejaculate. I was reading porn for knowledge, not to be sexually aroused. Thus, I would argue that for me as a preteen, porn had a socially redeeming value and was not just for becoming sexually excited. If I could have read the book without being excited, I would have done so, but I didn't have any control over the matter. This was also an important lesson in that I learned that sexual desire is an independent force beyond logic and reason.

After reading *Southern Sluts* over and over, I developed a theory of baby making (although no babies were actually made in the book), but I had learned my lesson and was not about to reduce my theory to the printed page. I called a meeting of my little group of subversive friends and gave them a lecture. This would be the start of another part of my life: the lecture circuit, or at least teaching and making speeches, something else that I have always enjoyed doing.

My friends were fascinated by my new theory. Most thought I was doing science fiction again, but when I produced my source material, they began to reevaluate my theory. I had highlighted a few key passages in the book and showed them to my friends. Interestingly enough, the girls intuited the truth of what I was saying, but most of the boys were still skeptical. Evidence that boys mature more slowly than girls and don't have anywhere near the level of intuition that girls have.

This knowledge came in handy in my adult career doing civil rights litigation where I often handled sexual harassment cases. For example, I once had a case where a male manager was accused of having an affair with a female subordinate and then discriminating against her in job assignments after the affair ended. He denied having the affair under oath in an affidavit and man to man in a private discussion with me. I interviewed eight coworkers in the office: five females and three males. All five females said yes the manager and female employee were definitely having an affair. All three males said, "No way."

Thus I wasn't shocked when just prior to the hearing, the employee's attorney produced love letters in the manager's handwriting, proving that they did indeed have an affair. Although the issue of employment discrimination was distinct from the issue of the affair, once the manager (whom I represented) was found to be a liar, he had no credibility on any issue, and settlement was our only option. The manager ended up crying on my shoulder and begging me to keep the case out of the news so that his wife didn't find out. We managed to keep it quiet, and he retired from his job. Men...

We will screw almost anything and tell almost any lie to try to cover it up—myself included. I have rarely lied, but when I have, it was related to sex: trying to get some, trying to cover up the fact that I got some, or pretending I had when I hadn't. Sexual deceit is multifaceted. Young, single men want their friends to think they are scoring left and right even when they aren't, married men want their wives to think they aren't scoring left and right when actually they are, and older men want their friends to think they are still having sex when they aren't (even with their wives).

I handled so many sexual harassment cases and heard so many lies that I accepted the cliché: when you ask a man about his sex life, you are asking to be lied to. A case in point was President Bill Clinton. I was certain from the beginning he was lying about not having sex "with that woman." Of course, he was going to lie. That's what men do. If every man who lied about sex lost his job, there wouldn't be many men employed: maybe a few kids on their first job at McDonald's and a few elderly men on their last job at Walmart but not many in the sexually active years, which seems to be roughly ages twelve to ninety.

My many years of dealing with litigation involving allegations of sexual harassment led to one of my second-rate murder mysteries: *Sexual Harassment Can Be Deadly*. This is the real title under my real name and is available at Amazon.com and Barnesandnoble.com. The novel is largely a true story with the names, dates, and places changed and a few murders added. It is a case of writing what I know and of the truth being stranger than fiction. Several people who read it thought the civil rights cases in it were too bizarre to be true, but every one of them was based on an actual case that I handled.

As most writers know, the truth is no defense for an unbelievable plotline. Some stories are so bizarre that the reader won't give them credibility or take them seriously even though they are 100 percent true. In those cases, the writer has to make the story more believable and less true to sustain credibility.

As they say, "Don't let the truth get in the way of a good story." Often this saying is used to justify adding fictional features, but it can also mean taking out true things that seem so bizarre as to make the story implausible.

I've used the same approach to this book. To the extent the book is not totally accurate, it is not because I have added fictional stories, but because I have left out some of the more incredulous true parts of my life.

CHAPTER 2

A Compulsion to Write

MUSICAL INTERLUDE:
"The Impossible Dream,"
from *Man of La Mancha*

Now that I'm more than seventy years old, I want to tell my last story while I can still can.
    Unfortunately, my memory is starting to fade, so I feel I must hurry before I forget everything. This may be Alzheimer's disease, some other form of dementia, or merely old age. It isn't terrible yet, but I notice a new problem every day. I had my DNA tested by 23andMe, and I have one of the e4 variants, which apparently makes Alzheimer's slightly more likely. One day I can't remember my cell phone number, another day I can't remember which month it is, and another I can't recall that I am meeting a friend for lunch.
    Here is the worst example. I put this book aside for over a year after my wife had a serious stroke. She couldn't talk or walk for a time, but a year later, after a lot of therapy, she was doing well. I decided I had better get back to this book

project if I ever intended to finish it. I had been dreading this phase—another edit—because I thought I had started the edit and then stopped twenty to thirty pages into it. However, when I returned to the book, I realized I had completed the entire edit of that draft. Either I am getting terribly forgetful or the writing fairy got into my computer and did more than two hundred pages of edits for me. Which is more likely?

While I have made a lot of money over the years from writing, it was always a secondary source of income. If I were writing only for money, I could have made much more by taking a second job at McDonald's or Walmart for minimum wage rather than putting thousands of hours into research, writing, rewriting, searching for an agent, and trying to find a publisher. It was never about the money. It was about my need to write—my genetic predisposition to write.

Financially, I'm pretty well off. I saved some money each payday, and I invest conservatively. I never trusted the stock market. It always seemed like a glorified pyramid scheme to me, with no more logic to winners and losers than the luck of the draw in Las Vegas, which is where I now live.

When I first heard about "selling short," I knew the stock market was just for gamblers and schemers. If you can make money when the market goes up *and* make money when it goes down, there is no reason for the rich, powerful, and connected to try to make the market go up. There are lots of reasons, however, for people to manipulate the market and make it go up and down and up and down, because they make money in both directions while the average investor (gambler) loses out. At least Vegas admits it's a crap shoot. Wall Street won't admit it, but it looks about the same to me.

There always seemed something slightly dishonorable about making money from investments. Sure, I have a 401(k)-type fund (you have little choice if you want to retire someday but to buy into this financial racket). Why should people make money off of money? It seems a built-in structural gimmick for the rich to get richer and leave everyone else behind. Systemic classism.

In any event, I worked for forty years and saved money, and I don't need to worry about it now. I can't use financial need as an excuse to keep writing. It's all about the genes and probably an environmental trigger.

What is the role of genes, and what is the role of society? As with many diseases, the disease (dis-ease) of writing probably requires both genetic and social components. My wife has multiple sclerosis (MS). The best thinking at present among neurologists is that people who get MS have a genetic predisposition and that there is then some type of environmental trigger. Both must have an impact for that person to develop MS.

This may also be the case for the writing malady. Those of us who are obsessed with writing probably have a genetic predisposition toward it and then are hit with some type of social or environment trigger. In my case, the trigger may have been the ability to sell those cowboy adventures to my third grade classmates. Had my early writing been rejected (as my fourth grade sex story was rudely rejected), I may have escaped from the clutches of this chronic obsession. Who knows?

I can't blame my parents. They were both readers but not writers. Strangely enough, although my mother was a teacher and might have seemed more intellectual than my father, she didn't read much literature. She rarely read fiction or anything beyond religious pamphlets, the *Ladies Home Journal,* and the Bible (which some might argue is the original best-selling work of fiction). My father, on the other hand, who never went to college and got a job in a factory after returning from World War II, read all the time: everything from murder mysteries, historical novels, and spy novels to biographies of presidents.

I got the love of reading from my parents, but I can't directly blame them for the writing addiction. It had to be a mutation.

I am often amazed when I think of the power of genetics and mutations. How else do I explain how a poor farm boy from an isolated, extremely conservative county in the Midwest, where no one dreamed of being a writer, grew up to be a liberal obsessed with writing who moved to New York City and then San Francisco as soon as he could afford to do so?

Musical Interlude:
"Born This Way," Lady Gaga

CHAPTER 3

A Writer's Point of View, or My First Tragedy

"We begin to live when we have conceived life as a tragedy."

—William Butler Yeats,
The Autobiography of William Butler Yeats

"Point of view" is a major topic in writing classes and books on writing, so I don't intend to spend any ink on it here in any traditional way. The point of view from which I normally write is dark and sad, with humor often used as a weapon against the darkness. Perhaps this is just another genetic predisposition, or perhaps I was warped by an early tragedy.

Humans are strange, and writers are stranger than most. They can take a tragedy, turn it into a story, and feel better about it.

W. Somerset Maugham, one of my favorite novelists, said that the best approach to life was one of "humorous resignation." I have generally taken that approach as well.

From an early age, life struck me as primarily a tragedy, and I have often used humor to deal with it. If this book seems to swing between comedy and tragedy (or at least attempts at them), it is because our lives are such a mixture.

When I was five years old, I was in love (well, more like a first crush) with a petite girl who lived nearby. Her name was Christine, but I called her Christy, and she called me Ronny. She was older than me and the cutest thing ever. We played together often.

Her mother had died shortly after she was born. "Mysteriously" was the word I heard people use when referring to it. I didn't know what the adults meant by mysteriously. I thought it was an unknown illness.

Her father was a drunk, but most of the time he was a nice guy. He would laugh and sing and sometimes play with Christy and me in their backyard, but on the weekends, he would drink, and I knew to stay away, because he was half crazy then.

On those days, Christy would come to my house to play. Sometimes other kids would show up. My cousins Billy and Donnie lived within walking distance. It was a rural area, but there were houses facing the road every few hundred yards with the farms and ranches in the back of the houses, so we weren't totally isolated, and we'd play Duck, Duck, Goose and other silly games.

I remember the moment I fell in love. Christy was wearing a peach-colored dress. I was in a cowboy outfit and riding Silver when Christy arrived in our backyard.

"Can I ride with you?" she asked. She had always been afraid of horses and had never asked to ride before.

"Sure. Climb up."

I rode over to the fence so she could climb aboard more easily. She sat in front of me. I was riding bareback as usual, as I was too lazy to put on a saddle. We rode around the field together, our little bodies touching and her long hair flying back into my face, smelling so fresh and clean. She giggled and said, "I'm not afraid if I'm with you."

In that instant, she went from being a playmate (who could have easily have been a boy) to being a girl whom I loved with all my heart and was determined to marry.

After this, we rode together on Silver many times. She had started school and would come to my house and share her great adventures with me after class. She thought I was too young to be her official boyfriend, but occasionally she let me give her a little kiss. She would laugh and call me her "silly boy." I don't think either of us had a clue about sex at this point—certainly I didn't. Even if someone had explained it to me, the concept would have seemed bizarre.

Christy had an old, hand-cranked Victrola that played huge 78 RPM records. We didn't have an electric record player in those ancient days of the mid-1950s. We'd wind up the Victrola and dance to "Tennessee Waltz" or something like that. I remember the cranking and the dancing more clearly than the music. It sounded scratchy and played at the wrong speed much of the time.

Christy was an excellent reader, and I started showing her a few of the stories I had written, printed on big yellow paper. She was encouraging. "These stories are great. You should write stories for the radio or TV."

This was an amazing suggestion. I understood that people wrote books, but it had never occurred to me that radio and TV stories were written. I naively thought they happened spontaneously, as if the actors on the radio made it up as they went along. We had limited TV in those days, and I had more experience with radio programs.

Christy often provided me with other insights. "Your stories always have happy endings. I like that. Life is so sad. Stories should be fun."

"Do you miss your mother?" I asked, thinking this was the main cause of her sadness.

"I don't remember her at all. Only from pictures. I do wish I had two parents like yours. They are so nice. My daddy isn't very nice sometimes. He hits me when he drinks."

This was something else I hadn't considered. I knew he shouted and acted mean sometimes, but I had never seen him hit her. This news made me furious. "If he hits you again, come over to our house. You can live with us."

"I'd like that. That would be a happy ending, like your stories."

After this, I wrote all my stories for Christy. She was my muse and my biggest fan (well, my only fan other than my mother), and I made sure all my stories had happy endings so that Christy liked them and liked me. She'd return one of my stories with high praise, often with key sentences highlighted in crayon, and say, "Write me another happy story." And I would, but her own life story didn't have a happy ending.

One Sunday afternoon, my parents and I were in the backyard playing croquet and listening to baseball on the radio. Harry Caray was broadcasting the St. Louis Cardinals. Harry was the world's greatest radio announcer and later became a legend on TV with the Cubs in Chicago, but for many years, we heard him from St. Louis on the radio. Dad was predicting the Cardinals would blow the game (he was always so pessimistic), but I thought from the sound of

Harry's optimistic voice that the Cardinals would hang on.

We were listening intently between croquet shots on the lawn when our phone rang. A phone call was a big deal in those days. We'd go weeks without one.

My father and mother gave each other a strange glance as if they were expecting bad news, and my dad quickly ran over and turned down the radio. I knew something was serious if we were turning off the game.

Dad answered our old-fashioned, crank-style phone and seemed upset. He said something like "it sounds like a gun shot." He had been in the war in the Pacific and hunted regularly. He came out of the house with a pistol, got in his car, and said he was going to Christy's house. I started to run after him, but my mother grabbed me and pulled me to the ground, falling over onto the lawn, shouting, "Stay here with me."

We waited for an hour. I wanted to go find out what was going on, but my mother held me tight. Our phone rang again (two calls in one day was unprecedented), and we went inside. My mother answered it while I watched from the hallway. She screamed, "Oh no," dropped the receiver to the floor, and slid down the wall to the floor, crying. While she hadn't said a word to explain what had happened, I knew it involved Christy.

We made it to Christy's house, but I don't remember how, since my father had our only car and Mom would not have driven a tractor that far. Maybe my grandfather gave us a ride.

When we arrived, Dad and several other people were in the yard of Christy's house. When he saw me running up, he scooped me up into his arms and said in a voice so calm but so sad it was chilling, "Don't go in there, son."

The sheriff arrived, and I listened in shock as my dad and the neighbor told what they had found. Christy had been shot dead by her drunken father who then killed himself. I remember my dad asking the sheriff, but I think he really was asking God, *Why did the bastard have to take her too?*

I can't remember anything about the next few days. I must have still been in shock. Even what I have written here may be partly wrong. Sometimes the whole thing seems like a nightmare that I have confused with a real event, but my parents discussed it with me periodically over the years, so I know it happened. I even have the newspaper clippings, but I have trouble recalling the events clearly. Did I go to her house? Did my father say that? The image of my mother on the phone, screaming, crying, and dropping to the floor is forever etched in my mind. I know that happened exactly the way I remember it, and that was when I knew for certain that something beyond horrible had happened.

The next event I clearly remember is the funeral some days later—probably the first funeral I ever attended, at least the first I recall. Christy's little body was in a coffin that seemed large enough for an adult. She wore her pink Sunday dress. The minister talked about how she was in heaven. For the first time, I asked myself but did not dare ask my parents, *How could God let this happen?* It was a thought that would linger for more than a decade until I accepted that God could be totally good or totally powerful but not both.

I wanted to believe in God then, and still do now, but I have struggled to find a definition that can exist in a world where such horrible things happen. If I must choose between an evil God and an ineffectual one, I'll go with inept. No one wants an evil God, but an ineffectual God isn't inspiring either.

Did Christy's murder make me an agnostic? Probably not. Given my logical tendencies, I might have become disillusioned with traditional religions anyway. This tragic event just gave me something to hang my first memories of doubt upon.

Memories are especially problematic for writers. Because Christy's murder had such an impact on my life, I used that incident in several versions of short stories and novels. These were all fictionalized to one degree or another and all different, so years after the real event, I have trouble remembering precisely what did happen beyond the obvious: she was murdered by her father who then killed himself.

This was the first tragic event in my life. I was just days from my sixth birthday and have thought of it often. More than sixty-five years later, I still miss her. The rest are peripheral details.

There were other tragedies when I was young—my cousin Donnie died in a car crash when he was sixteen, and a classmate, Jimmy, drowned at seventeen on our senior trip to Washington—but nothing hit me harder than the tragedy with Christy.

I do recall a few weeks after the funeral I was finally able to get into Christy's old house. I had become obsessed with wondering if she ever read my last story and if they were the last words she read. I was so afraid I would find it covered in blood, but I found it in the drawer by her bed with no signs of blood or damage or any crayon marks. Did she ever get to read it? I'll never know.

CHAPTER 4

Another Embarrassing Failure

Writers often go into seclusion, withdraw from the world, or develop severe writer's block after a bad experience, and this is exactly what happened to me after being interrogated about my fourth grade sex story. I didn't write any stories for a few years. The money (the pennies and nickels) wasn't worth the humiliation of having to retract my story and admit that I didn't know what the heck I was talking about.

Then, in sixth grade, I learned about the joys of being a ghostwriter. Students could receive extra credit writing additional book reports. I never bothered, as I was an A student anyway, but the class bully, Jack, was always on the verge of failing. He and I were not friends, but we did play sports together. He never hassled me, as he respected my athletic ability and liked to be on my team when sides were chosen, as my team often won. One day, he asked me if I'd help him by writing some of his book reports so he could pass. With a combination of humanitarian benevolence (I did sort of like the guy, as our grandmothers were friends) and fear that if I said no he'd break my legs, I agreed.

I wrote about books I had already read—*Animal Farm*, *The Wonderful Wizard of Oz*, and the like—so it didn't cost me much time, and I saved Jack from failing. Over the years, I occasionally bailed him out when he needed a written report, and he bailed me out by beating the crap out of any one who dared to hassle me in any way. It was the beginning of a beautiful relationship. Word got around that if you messed with Ron, you messed with Jack, and soon, no one ever messed with Ron or Jack. Writing was beginning to have a positive impact on my life again.

Still, I realized by middle school that while writers may appeal to women (at this stage, "girls") in some indirect, roundabout way, most of the girls, and especially the cheerleaders, were more interested in sports stars. My middle school years were focused on basketball, not writing. When I was in eighth grade, I was a starter, and we won a local championship. I had a nice girlfriend who helped me celebrate in a nice way but not "all the way."

Ironically, I wouldn't get beyond second base with a girl until I went away to Christian camp. Arcadia was a Christian summer camp experience combining singing, dancing, boating, swimming, and some time each day to praise Jesus. I was about to be a freshman in high school when I went, and while my knowledge of sex had progressed from the disastrous "Babies and Storks: Myth or Reality" days, I still didn't have a full understanding of the preliminary process. There was only so much information you could get from books—a living human female body was needed to fill in lots of experiential details.

The camp was for high school students from a wide area of the state of Missouri. We ranged from freshmen to seniors, and most of us didn't know each other. While I was a fourteen-year-old boy, I was tall and looked older, so I lied and said I was seventeen and a junior. The only person there who knew me was my cousin Billy, and he was pumping out more bull than I was and wasn't going to blow my cover.

An eighteen-year-old senior-to-be named Kathy took a liking to me. Each night she and I gathered around the campfire (about a hundred of us in all) and sang "Kum Ba Ya." Although it was summer, the weather was cool at night on Iron Mountain, and we often brought blankets. Kathy and I bundled up under her blanket and sang "Michael, Row the Boat Ashore" and other campfire classics.

We started by holding hands, but by the second night, Kathy put my hands under the blanket and up her blouse so that I could fondle her naked breasts without anyone noticing. I would never have had the nerve to initiate this on my own, but she put my hands on her boobs, smiled, and said, "Nice, huh?"

I smiled and said, "Absolutely," and I wasn't lying. She had large, firm breasts, and it was great fun playing with them. I felt like I was in heaven and had no trouble shouting out a few "Thank you, Jesus!" lines from time to time.

The only downside to this arrangement was that I couldn't see her breasts. I could caress them, but they were still hidden. The next night, we graduated to a walk in the woods, and there I got to see what I was touching. They were magnificent. By the fourth night, we were swimming nude in the lake and rubbing our bodies together to stay warm. I had dreaded the thought of going to camp when my parents forced me to go, and now I wanted camp to last for years. I was truly in heaven, but the two weeks ended all too soon.

Kathy went back to her town, and I went back to mine, about sixty miles away. I started to write again—not stories but fiction all the same. She thought I was a seventeen-year-old junior. I wrote her a love letter every day or two and filled in details about my life as a junior, and she wrote me lovely letters about her senior year. I don't know what insanity made me think I could continue to get away with this. Perhaps it was the overriding desire to see her lovely body again, so I wrote and wrote.

Even the best writing can hide outright lies for only so long—ask President George W. Bush's speechwriter. Eventually reality shows up to bite you in the ass.

One night, Kathy surprised me and came to one of my high school basketball games where the program listed me accurately as six foot three and a freshman. She was furious that I had lied about my age. She left without talking to me.

In fact, I didn't even know she had been there until I got her letter (her last letter ever) a few days later, telling me what a scoundrel I was and how she never wanted to see or hear from me again. I wrote her a dozen or more times, trying to apologize and explain my lies as best I could, but she never replied, and I never saw her again. She probably never even read my letters. Such is my fate; so much of what I write, no one ever reads.

CHAPTER 5

Discovering Female and African American Authors (1963)

Meanwhile back in high school, since I no longer was writing love letters to Kathy every night or two, I had time to write other things. I was in an advanced English class where I could get extra credits for creative writing. I started pumping out poems and a couple of short stories every week.

Then, I had some injuries and health issues and had to give up basketball, which gave me even more time to write. This is when writing became my obsession again in a strange way.

Since I wasn't able to play basketball, I ended up with an extra study hall at the end of the day. It was populated mainly with senior girls. One day, I happened to sit at a table with a senior named Cindy Sue. She was a gorgeous redhead, so I flirted, and we talked. She noticed me writing a short story for my class and mentioned that she hated writing, could never come up with any ideas, and was in danger of failing her class and not graduating.

"Hey, I love to write," I said without any forethought. "Maybe I could help you."

"You'd do that?" She smiled and winked.

I was hooked. Over the next few weeks, I wrote several stories for her to turn in as her own. Suddenly, she went from a D- to a solid B. Hanging out with Cindy Sue in seventh-hour study hall became my favorite part of the day.

It turned out ghostwriting, or whatever literary name you may put on my unethical activities, wasn't my thing either. The first five or six stories I wrote for her got her A's and B's, but her teacher became suspicious. She was interrogated, and she cracked and confessed. I was once again called to the principal's office to meet with him and Cindy Sue's English teacher, Mrs. Barks. The only positive thing I can say for Cindy Sue was she did have the decency to have a mutual friend slip me a note and warn me about what had happened, so when I got to the principal's office, I knew the cat was already out of the bag.

I confessed and didn't compound my problems by telling the principal lies.

"How long did you think you could get away with this?" the principal asked.

Having been honest thus far, and knowing that the principal was himself a ladies man who wasn't above hitting on the senior girls himself once they were over eighteen, I decided to be straight. "Long enough to sleep with her."

The principal laughed, but the English teacher didn't. She looked offended.

I turned my attention to her. "How did you know it wasn't her?" I asked Mrs. Barks.

She straightened her back and gave me a rigid look, but then, happy to pontificate, replied, "Lots of reasons. Cindy Sue had never been a good writer before. The vocabulary was way beyond anything I ever heard her use, and the more stories I read, although they were about girls and things a girl would be interested in, the more I was certain a man had written the stories. They had that male perspective and didn't sound at all like a girl would have written them. I didn't know it was you. I thought maybe her brother or even a boyfriend in college, but I was sure it was a male."

This was a startling insight for my little mind. It had never occurred to me that one could deduce the gender of the writer from the manner of writing. I understood my stories couldn't just be about sports, and I had written about romantic and feminine subjects when pretending to be Cindy Sue, but I was amazed that my gender was still so evident.

Okay, in retrospective, it is obvious. Men and women write differently, not just about different subjects but with different styles and tones and with different insights, but to a fourteen-year-old, this was a remarkable revelation.

I began thinking about books I'd read and realized that I rarely read anything by a female author. From the first book I was exposed to in church and Sunday school—the Bible, which even I could deduce was written by men, not due to its style but to its obvious low regard for women—to every book assigned to me so far in high school (Shakespeare, Edgar Allan Poe, Walt Whitman, Ernest Hemingway, F. Scott Fitzgerald, and so forth).

Virtually everything I read was written by a man including the daily news, the sports pages of the *St. Louis Post-Dispatch*, and even my comic book adventures. Where were the female writers? Why didn't our English teacher (a woman) assign us any female authors?

Getting caught writing short stories for the lovely Cindy Sue had two immediate effects. First, she dumped me. Since

I could no longer help her with her homework, she moved on to a college boyfriend, and my little stories never did get me into her pants. The most I ever got from her were a few kisses and an occasional handful of her delightful breasts in the coatroom. I never got a real date with her, in part, because at fourteen, I couldn't yet drive.

Second, I became temporarily obsessed with reading female authors. I went to the high school library where the only female author was Agatha Christie. I read a couple of her mysteries, which were lots of fun but not especially enlightening about gender. I tried the city library and discovered Kate Chopin's *The Awakening*. This book was amazing. I couldn't believe it was in the city library. Probably the only reason they had it was because Chopin was from St. Louis, it was a famous book, and the librarians hadn't read it.

This book, as I understood it at fourteen, was about a woman who wanted to be free so badly that she abandoned her husband and children to have a life of her own. Wow! I hadn't decided if she was a hero, a villain, or a bit of both, but she was someone worth reading about. It was an awakening for me.

After reading Chopin, I wanted to read female authors more than ever, but it wasn't that easy to find much more in the local libraries other than picture books for little kids. It was back to the bookstore on Broadway in Cape Girardeau. At least they had female authors, and I didn't need to have my wino friend buy them for me. I started with Virginia Woolf but realized she was way over my head and put her aside until years later.

I found a collection of stories by Dorothy Parker in a used book section, got hooked, and read every one. She had such a delightful sense of humor.

I went on to read all the female authors I could: Mary Shelley, Jane Austen, Harriet Beecher Stowe, Julia Ward Howe, Louisa May Alcott, Anne Bronte, Emily Dickinson (who I admit I often found difficult), and many more. I read Anne Frank's *The Diary of a Young Girl*, which was difficult in a different sense, in that I kept crying every few pages. I had to read it at home, as I didn't want to be seen crying in study hall. It would have ruined what little was left of my macho image. Everyone would have thought I was crying over being dumped by Cindy Sue, although in truth, I did still feel like crying over her, especially Friday afternoons when her college boyfriend picked her up after study hall in his little blue MG convertible.

Then, I stumbled upon *A Spy in the House of Love* by Anais Nin. After reading it, I thought she was the best female writer in the world, because she was both smart and sexy. Years later, I read all her diaries and erotica. She was my first literary crush.

After reading several female authors, it occurred to my slow brain that I had never read anything by a black author. Again, I started my search in the school library, and there was nothing. They at least had a few books by women, but for black writers, there was zilch.

The city library was a little better. The only black writer I had heard much about was Martin Luther King, Jr. I started with him, reading *Stride Toward Freedom: The Montgomery Story* and *Why We Can't Wait*.

I moved on to novels. I especially liked James Baldwin's *Go Tell It on the Mountain* and Ralph Ellison's *Invisible Man*, but the book that blew me away was W. E. B. Du Bois' *The Souls of Black Folk*. It was brilliant and so powerful. I was stunned to realize it had been written in 1903. How was it possible that sixty years later my school didn't have a copy of it? It should have been required reading in my all-white community. It still should be today.

My little town has undergone a sad transition in terms of race. When I was a child, race was never an issue in our immediate area; there were no black people within twenty-five miles of my house. When I was a teenager, thanks to television, we all became aware of the civil rights movement, and strangely enough, our local church supported it. My father was president of the church board, and we sent money and volunteer marchers to support Dr. King.

Looking back from today, this blows my mind. That community is probably 90 percent Trump supporters now, and some people there do not hesitate to use the "n" word publicly. The last time I drove through the village, I saw two confederate flags flying. What the hell happened?

Well, I don't know. I left the area when I was seventeen and didn't witness the transition on a firsthand basis, but I have a theory. In the early 1960s, the all-white community where I lived perceived black people in the South primarily as fellow Christians. Dr. King was a Christian minister, as were Reverend Jackson and Reverend Abernathy. When the rednecks in the South started bombing churches and killing children, that was clearly the work of evil people. Good Christians were being denied their right to worship. It was an easy decision to support black Christians who wanted equal rights and the ability to attend church without being killed. My little church sent money and encouraged volunteers (including me) to support the civil rights movement.

Now more than fifty years later, many rural white communities don't see black people as fellow Christians, or fellow humans, but as criminals and welfare cheats living high off the taxes white people pay. How did this occur? I think we can put much of the blame on Richard Nixon and his Southern Strategy. This started in 1968 and continued through Donald Trump as the Republicans decided to be the White Male Party. The Repugs have done an effective job of convincing small-town white people that black people are evil in some manner or other and that only Republicans can stop black crime and prevent black people from ripping off the welfare and healthcare systems.

The Republicans were afraid of a class war wherein poor and middle-class whites would join with blacks and demand the rich pay their share of taxes. They started a race war to distract white people from their real political enemies: the super rich.

Today, there are more good black writers than ever. I recently finished reading *Tears We Cannot Stop* by Michael Eric Dyson. It made me want to cry myself, thinking how it is unlikely to change anything, given our president at the time (Trump) was too stupid to read a book, much less understand it and do something positive to help people. Another great modern writer is Ijeoma Oluo, whose book *Mediocre: The Dangerous Legacy of White Male America* is one of the best critiques of America's past and present that I have read.

CHAPTER 6

Becoming a Sportswriter

Still, back in high school, with all this reading, I stopped writing. This is an eternal dilemma for writers: How much do we read compared to how much we write? We have to read to learn about the world and technique, but if we don't stop reading at some point, we never get around to writing anything.

I spent the summer between my freshman and sophomore years reading books by female and black authors (and playing lots of baseball with my friends), but as my sophomore year started, I went back to writing short stories for extra credit.

One story about my wonderful Grandmother Grace so impressed my teacher that she submitted it to a statewide contest for high school writers. I again got all excited about becoming a writer, but I didn't win.

Rejection is something with which writers have to deal. For every writing success I've had, there were a dozen rejections. It hurts. Time after time, people tell you that your writing is worthless. You've spent weeks, months, or, on a book-length project, years writing and rewriting it to be perfect, and then everyone says it's unreadable trash, and often they are right. It still hurts.

How do you go on? Sometimes you don't.

I gave up writing and went back to basketball. Unfortunately, I was a sophomore and couldn't play on the freshman team (where I could have been a star) and had to play on the varsity team where I wasn't good enough to be a starter. I was tall and could shoot better than anyone on the team, but I was light and got pushed around a lot under the basket. I had lots of minor injuries that kept me sidelined much of the time. When the season ended, I switched to baseball, which had much less physical contact and fewer injuries. I was a decent pitcher due to throwing a fairly good knuckleball.

I found a new girlfriend and started writing love poems for her. She thought I was a genius and encouraged my writing. She loved everything I wrote as long as it was about her. You might impress a girl with a story, but you can't keep her with a story.

By junior year, I had come to the sad realization that I would never be a professional baseball or basketball player. I decided to be a sportswriter instead, since I loved sports and writing. I gave up playing sports and became the team's official scorer, which got me close access to all the games plus a ride on the team bus. I wrote up the game summaries for the paper.

Even the simplest article about a regular season high school basketball game can be controversial. Every player wanted to be the star. Everyone wanted press. My cousin Bill was the real star of the team, but I was accused of giving him preferential treatment by boasting about his exploits. Once I was accused of improper recordkeeping in the scorebook to try to help him set a scoring record, which was untrue, but everyone loves to criticize a writer, and when they can't find one thing to complain about, they'll find another.

Still, I was writing regularly for the paper, and people were reading it if only to find fault. I was hanging out with other "writers"—that is, other nerds who also wrote for the paper. One of the nerds was a cute sophomore girl, and soon we were dating. It was the first time I had dated someone who also liked to write.

Terri and I wrote stories and critiqued each other. This was fun at first, but she became too critical, and I was offended. I became overly critical of her stories, and next thing you know, we broke up. Ever since, I have been afraid to get seriously involved with another writer.

I have the same fear of so-called writer's support groups. They say these groups can provide support and constructive criticism, but the few I have tried didn't turn out well. The constructive criticism quickly turns into bitchy criticism. The most successful writer in the group (never me) becomes a pompous lecturer, or the less successful writers gang up on anyone with a margin of success no matter how limited. I hate to criticize the work of others, because I know how hard they toil to produce even the most banal stories. I prefer to let the publishers, editors, and agents burst their writing bubbles rather than be the bad guy. Besides, what the hell do I know? Some of the worst crap not only gets published but becomes a best seller.

Senior year was just junior year the sequel. I was the sportswriter for the paper. Girlfriends came, and girlfriends went. By the end of the year, I was reduced to dating a freshman.

This was humbling. I had often dated or been romantically involved with older girls, but now I was a senior and dating a girl just out of middle school. The older girls, especially the cheerleaders, wanted the sports *stars*. They didn't want a sportswriter. I was seen by these sophisticated beauties as something of a loser. Writers got no respect. Even today, I don't think writers get the babes unless they are successful screenwriters in Hollywood, and even there, I bet the actors do much better than the writers.

I kept reminding myself that Marilyn Monroe married a writer, Arthur Miller. Of course, she was also involved with a great baseball player and a president. If I was going to date the sex symbol of my generation, it was clear which one of the three professions I had the best chance at.

Although she was a freshman, Janey was well developed for her age (I was seventeen, she was fourteen). She thought I was a genius and would eventually win the Pulitzer Prize. She loved every word I wrote, even my silly sports summaries in the paper. I was in love…yet again. It wasn't the sex. We never had sex. She was too fearful of pregnancy, but oh how that girl could kiss. Nights at the drive-in movies were like being in heaven.

There was one big problem: she was Catholic. She was the only Catholic person in our school from the only Catholic family in our little town. I don't recall how the family even ended up in our hick village on the outskirts of Cape Girardeau, which was a city of fewer than fifty thousand in those days. I think her father had something to do with monitoring a gas or oil pipeline.

Our little town was 100 percent WASP. There were no blacks, Hispanics, Catholics, Jews, or Asians. In 1960, when Kennedy ran for president, our minister preached from the pulpit against him, arguing that he was not "a real American" and that his allegiance would be to the Pope in Rome, not to the United States. Given this view of Catholics, you can imagine how people in the area felt about Janey's family. Probably the way they would look at a Muslim family these days.

My parents lit the match by pressuring me to stop seeing her, but the real fireworks were in Sunday school. I was a high school senior, but I still went to Sunday school every week in part to appease my parents and in part to hang out with my friends. Our teacher was the minister's wife, a cute little bimbo who I liked until one Sunday when she started in on how everyone other than Christian Protestants was doomed to hell. This included Buddhists, Hindus, Jews, Muslims, non-believers, and, of course, Catholics.

I protested. There was an argument. I used a few words not normally heard in Sunday school, certainly not in the context that I used them and certainly not directed at the minister's wife. I was asked to leave the class and did so. I was told that I had to publicly apologize or be expelled. I refused to apologize.

My parents blamed my poor conduct (okay, I did use inappropriate language, and suggesting the minister's wife could "go to hell" may have been over the line) on my relationship with Janey and insisted I stop seeing her. I refused. They cut off my allowance. I moved out and went to live with my grandparents. My grandmother was a saint. She supported anything I did. She didn't know the difference between a Catholic, a Hindu, and a Lutheran (we were Methodist), but she knew I was her grandson and could do no wrong. No wonder I loved her so much. She let me live in her guest bedroom for a few weeks until my parents settled down.

I continued to see Janey, and I didn't return to a traditional Christian church for more than half a century. I had always found Christianity to be illogical but thought as I got older I would understand it better. Now that I had been expelled, I was glad to be away from all that irrational nonsense.

I started exploring other religions. I read everything I could by Alan Watts and became interested in Buddhism and Eastern philosophy. I read *On the Road* by Kerouac and discovered J. D. Salinger, reading *Catcher in the Rye* (still one of the funniest books I've ever read), *Franny and Zooey*, and everything else he wrote, including the short stories.

I gave up on being a sportswriter (sports seemed so trivial to me by then) and decided to become the next J. D. Salinger. Fat chance! I didn't realize that there were already about a million writers out there dreaming of being the next Salinger.

CHAPTER 7

The 1960s: Sex, Drugs, and Radical Student Newspapers

A few months later, I went away to college, and Janey and I drifted apart. I wrote her love letters almost daily, but prolonged distance during the teen years is almost always fatal to romance. I got caught up in the political movements of the 1960s: civil rights, anti-war, and especially free love. Janey and I stayed friends and pen pals over all these decades, but we went our separate ways.

Having decided to be the next Salinger, I initially majored in English literature. I got a D in my first class. I had never received a D before. I was in shock. The professor saw everything as symbolic, and his symbols and mine didn't match. Poetry was the worst. He could read ten meanings into some inconsequential, three-word phrase. I thought his class was all bull.

Even the novels resulted in disagreement. The professor felt that *Don Quixote* was a symbolic attack on fascism, Nazism, and Franco's Spain. I asked how this was possible since Cervantes wrote his classic centuries before any of those dreadful political systems came into existence. The professor didn't answer directly. He never did. Instead, he accused me of having no "symbolic sensitivity."

His class was an exercise in "creative" interpretations of classic novels and poems. Of course, my interpretation was always wrong (even though I often stole mine directly from CliffsNotes), and his was always right. I got the D and began to have doubts about being a literature major.

Revolution was in the air, and writing, at least writing anything other than political polemics, seemed a waste of time. I switched to political science, made A's with minimal difficulty, and spent much of my time hanging out with political activists who were equally interested in making love and stopping wars—my kind of crowd.

The University of Mediocre Missouri was a conservative place, but even here there were thousands of students ready to seize a building or burn a bra to protest something or other. We weren't always sure what, why, or how. We decided we needed our own newspaper, something to counter the official school paper that printed only right-wing propaganda and articles on pig farming. (No joke—we had lots of agriculture majors who loved to beat up hippies.)

We started a weekly counterculture newspaper called *Mo News Than Is Fit to Print*, playing off the line from *The New York Times* and the abbreviation for Missouri, turning it into *mo*, which we thought was a clever variation of *more*. We thought it was a great name, but most students hated it, so we changed it six times the first year. I can't remember all of them. One was *Students for a Sane Society*, which sounded more like a student mental health group than a paper. One was *Stop, Read, and Think*. We settled on *Revolution Number Nine* after a bizarre Beatles' song from their recent *The White Album*, mainly because everyone in the group liked John Lennon. The buzz was he and Yoko wrote that song over the objections of Paul McCartney, and the song seemed to signify revolt in many perspectives.

Despite all the name changes, our readership increased dramatically each week, and we had to keep printing more copies. While the paper was free, we asked for donations to be mailed to our post office box and received lots of funds, more than enough to keep rolling.

The University of Muddled Missouri had an outstanding journalism school, and we tapped some talent among the faculty and students. They gave us some professional cachet we would not have had otherwise. I ended up as the main editor of the newsletter, primarily because I was willing to sink a lot of my personal time into the project. Hard work never hurts, and as editor, I had a major influence on what we published each week, so I could always include a couple of my diatribes.

Being a sportswriter for high school basketball had not helped me much with the female crowd, but being the editor and chief rabble-rouser for a counterculture college paper brought women out of the woodwork, writing me daily and asking to meet for coffee. (I was only twenty and couldn't legally drink). Many sent photos. Some wore bikinis, some even less. I accepted as many of the offers as I could. It was too good to last.

Our newspaper (okay, some issues were more like pamphlets and some little more than a two-page flyer) became a rallying point. We helped facilitate protests, rallies, and anti-war activities. The university struck back. We had never been an official campus publication, but the faculty were ordered to stop assisting us. They claimed the newspaper was a "communist-inspired paper promoting the overthrow of the United States government" and shut us down. The ACLU didn't think our little publication was worth defending but referred us to a local attorney who'd work for free. She came to our defense. The threat of legal action against the university was enough to get them to back down, but the process took four months. By the time we were allowed to resume publishing, many of our contributors and supporters had moved on, several to other projects, or left campus.

I had lost interest in the project as well. I admit it—young people have short attention spans. I certainly did. By the early 1970s, I had a bachelor's degree in political science and was continuing with my postgraduate program—part law, part master's in poly sci—but the big change was the draft lottery.

I lucked out and received a safe number, so the war in Vietnam was no longer an immediate threat to my survival. The same fortunate fate fell to some of my friends, and we lost much of our motivation to protest the war. We still went through the motions and attended the anti-war rallies, but the passion (or fear?) was gone.

We published a couple issues of the revived newspaper just to piss off the administration, but soon we started to cut back. We went to once a month, then once a quarter, and then the paper faded away without a formal decision ever having been made to stop publication. Other younger radicals had started a much less provocative alternative paper when we were shut down, and they had the bigger following on campus, so my radical newspaper days came to an end.

Musical Interlude:
"Those Were the Days," Mary Hopkin

CHAPTER 8

Mapping New York State

Musical Interlude:
"Follow That Dream," Elvis Presley
"He Went to Paris," Jimmy Buffett
"New York, New York," Liza Minnelli

I completed my studies as fast as I could and decided it was time to go out into the so-called real world and get a job. I finished the work on my master's degree, but law school was too long and time-consuming. I was ready for a complete change of pace.

I had taken the civil service exam, and since I always did well on tests, I scored high and started getting job offers from all over the nation. Most of them were seeking security officers on airlines. This was when the biggest airline security problem was planes being hijacked to Cuba and long before Islamic militants got into the game. I had no desire to shoot it out with a hijacker at thirty-five thousand feet, so I passed on those offers.

Then, I got a job offer with the Social Security Administration in Buffalo, New York. It sounded interesting, but my real interest was in New York City. I saw myself as a young writer living in Manhattan and becoming the next J. D. Salinger after all. It seemed that no matter how hard or how often I tried to quit writing and move on to something else, at the slightest suggestion or inspiration (even if only in my own head), I resumed my fantasy of being a writer. It was an obsession I never got over.

I accepted the job without knowing what the work would be or where Buffalo was. I vaguely thought it was a suburb of New York City until I looked on the map and was astonished to see the cities were several hundred miles apart. Still, this assignment was only for the twelve-week training class. I was assured that my permanent assignment would be in the New York metro area, so I spent a summer in Buffalo. What I most remember were some lovely evenings in nearby Niagara Falls with a sensuous woman from my training class.

Soon I'd be on to New York City and fame and fortune at Simon & Schuster, appearances on *The Tonight Show*, and a book tour of Europe. Nope.

The first disappointment was that I didn't get the office in midtown Manhattan that I had requested but was assigned to a town called Elmira, which I had never heard of until the moment our assignments were announced. Again, I had to look on a map to see where it was. It was a long way from Manhattan, sitting on the New York-Pennsylvania border south of Ithaca, home of Cornell University.

My displeasure over the assignment was mitigated by the fact that a beautiful woman in the class was also assigned to Elmira. Her name was Judy. She and I had been cordial during the class, but I had been dating someone else. Now that it looked like we would be going to this small city together, we started hanging out. The rest is matrimonial history.

In early October, Judy and I moved to Elmira. We kept separate apartments but spent virtually every evening together. Most weekends we drove down to New York City to explore museums and go to the theater. On Thanksgiving weekend, we moved in together, and by January 1972, we were married. We spent our wedding night going to see *Fiddler on the Roof* and staying at the Waldorf Astoria, and we went to Europe for our honeymoon. We have been married, happily most of the time, for more than forty-nine years.

My personal life in Elmira was good, and Elmira had connections to some famous authors such as Mark Twain, who is buried there, but I wasn't writing at all. Judy and I were making love two or three times a night, and there just wasn't much time or energy for anything else. The job turned out to be time consuming. I had thought I might be like Einstein, Hawthorne, or Walt Whitman, men who worked bland civil service jobs to pay the bills and still had plenty of time each day to write (or in Einstein's case, to develop new theories), but this job, which involved interviewing elderly people applying for Social Security benefits, took up my day and left me no free time.

Then, we got lucky. We were hit by a hurricane. In June 1972, Hurricane Agnes struck the East Coast. New York State and Pennsylvania took it hard. The Chemung River in Elmira flooded and destroyed most of the downtown area, including our office. Judy and I happened to have an apartment on the far western side of town, largely because initially we had lived together unmarried and didn't want people in the office to know. The federal government still frowned upon cohabitation in the early 1970s. We were able to drive away from the flood zone, where all the other employees were stranded and without phone service, and report to another Social Security office in Auburn, New York. This resulted in us becoming the only contacts between the destroyed Elmira office and the top managers in the regional office in New York City.

Management was impressed by our commitment to duty in reporting to another office for work during the emergency. Actually, we just wanted to be somewhere with electricity and drinkable water, but we never admitted that. Within a few months, we were offered promotions and relocation to jobs in New York City.

Soon we were living in the Big Apple, and I thought it was only a matter of time until I became a famous writer. The job in New York was as a paper pusher and more along the lines of what I wanted. I could do my work in about three hours each day and still be the most productive employee in my unit, and that left me five hours a day for writing. I thought just being in New York City would make the publishers want to publish my books and articles or at least read them and give me helpful hints. Wrong again.

Publishers were unimpressed by my New York City mailing address. The entire time I lived in NYC, I never had anything published, and only a few of my manuscripts received a second glance. It was frustrating. I must have collected three hundred rejection slips a year. Some were polite ("It's not for us, better luck elsewhere"), some were quick ("sorry" written on my query letter and returned in my SASE), and some were downright mean ("This sounds like a lackluster project that would be impossible to market").

Meanwhile, life in New York City in the early 1970s turned out to be a huge hassle. Judy and I couldn't afford the insurance and parking to own a car, so we took public transportation everywhere. There were frequent fights and shootouts in the subways, and we were always alert to being mugged and riding the one subway car with a transit policeman. The grocery stores were small, inconvenient, and overpriced. Taxicabs, just like the cliché, were never around when you needed one. Everything was dirty and depressing. It wasn't at all like the movies from the 1940s and 1950s. How did Doris Day afford that nice apartment in Manhattan on a secretary's salary?

Judy disliked her job (the same job as mine but in a different unit). Since she wasn't a writer, she had nothing to do all day to appear to be busy except do actual work, which was boring, and the irritations of life in NYC were starting to wear her down. We got a chance for jobs in San Francisco. We flew out for interviews and both fell in love with the city and the Bay Area. It was and remains our idea of heaven on earth.

They offered us jobs, and we accepted. I had other literary heroes from the Bay Area: Alan Watts, Lawrence Ferlinghetti, Allen Ginsberg, Richard Brautigan, Dashiell Hammett, and Armistead Maupin. I would hang out at the City Lights Bookstore and change my fantasy to fit a new scenario. I didn't have to live in NYC to be a writer.

CHAPTER 9

California in the 1970s
(The Wild, Wild West of the Sexual Frontier)

MUSICAL INTERLUDE:
"California Dreamin'," The Mamas & the Papas
"California," Melissa Etheridge

We loved the Bay Area. We got a great apartment at a place called Watergate (named before the Nixon scandal) on San Francisco Bay with a great view of the city and the Golden Gate Bridge. San Francisco was still much cheaper than New York in those days (1974), so we had a car again and a great lifestyle. I was inspired by our beautiful surroundings to write some awful books.

I wrote a horrible sci-fi novel called "The Dark Side of the Moon." A couple of editors read it and suggested that I not quit my day job. They were right. It was terrible. I didn't know enough about science to write science fiction. In the end, I burned it in a ritual sacrifice to the muse on a night of the full moon.

I wrote another novel called "The Scream," inspired by

the painting of the same name by Edvard Munch (which later sold for more than two hundred million dollars, a few million more than my book earned, I'm afraid). I thought the book was a scream, but the editors thought it was more of a nightmare. I collected many more rejection slips and suggestions that perhaps I should read more and live more before writing more.

In the mid-1970s, Judy and I decided on a trial separation for reasons unrelated to writing and largely related to my desire to make love to every pretty woman in California. I wanted the full California experience. I was in my twenties, tall, healthy, fit, and blond (sun bleached). Women were hitting on me by the dozens, and I wanted to take full advantage.

I guess sex is my main vice. I don't smoke, get drunk, or gamble, rarely cuss, don't use hard drugs, and am never violent. My lifestyle is so tame that if not for my obsession with women, I could have been an Anglican parson in Victorian England.

In the 1970s, I moved into a tiny studio apartment right on San Francisco Bay. It was the wildest time of my life. I was able to stay up twenty hours a day and survive with only four hours of sleep thanks to massive amounts of caffeine. I wrote ten hours a day, mostly while pretending to work in the office, and partied ten hours a day. I was living alone in San Francisco in the 1970s amid the peak of the sexual revolution. I had women left and right. Well, in the Bay Area, they were all left. Not many right-wingers in this progressive haven.

I don't want to sound like some Don Juan. Everyone was screwing everyone in the midseventies in California, so it was easy to find a hookup. All you needed was a pulse.

This was after the pill but before AIDS or even herpes, so hooking up didn't require much talent. The only limit was one's physical stamina, not the lack of willing partners. It was a hedonist's paradise. It was the wild, wild West of the sexual frontier. It was the Golden Age of sexual freedom. I had always been fairly lucky with women. Although I am mainly an introvert, women often come on to me, and in the seventies in California, it was like a tidal wave of women coming at me. I could not have gotten away from it if I had wanted to, and I didn't want to.

As one example, there was a cute woman named Doris in our office with whom I was friendly but never flirted because her husband also worked in our office (we had more than two thousand employees in our building). I spoke with him on a couple of occasions, and he was obsessed with scuba diving. It was all he wanted to talk about, and it was boring after a few minutes. Doris was interested in literature, so we had more in common. Still, I had no reason to think she was interested in me sexually. Late one night, she showed up at my apartment, invited herself in, and asked, "Can I spend the night with you?"

I was shocked, as I didn't realize she even knew where I lived. I stalled by asking, "Aren't you still married to Jack?"

"Yes, but all he wants to do is go diving in the ocean. I want a man who wants to dive into me, and I've heard around that you are the kind of guy who will not turn a lady down."

"Well, you've heard right, and you've come to the right place."

We did a lot of diving for five days. Then, it was over as fast as it started. She said, "I love this, but I want it all the time, not just now and then." She divorced Jack, moved to

Washington, DC, to start a new career, and found a new husband who enjoyed her version of diving. Despite our all-too-brief affair, we have remained friends to this day.

I have remained friends with the majority of my former long-term lovers. I think it is because after my bad experience with Kathy at Christian camp, when I lied about my age, I never again lied to one of my lovers.

There were so many women wanting a good time—mainly single or divorced, but several in open marriages and even one in an open group marriage. Becky had two husbands and still had time and energy for a lover. She could do tricks I have never seen before or since. Another woman had just left a sex commune and complained she "wasn't getting enough sex" there. She later moved to Nevada and got a job in one of the legal brothels, as apparently she just wanted to have sex all the time.

One divorced woman who was older and a little overweight seduced me just with her soft, sexy voice. This was the first time I had ever slept with a woman who had had a child, which was just an issue because she could never get a babysitter at night and kept warning me to be quiet so as not to wake her son, and yet it was her soft voice that turned to loud screams during sex that kept waking him up. After a few weeks, she noted I was not "stepfather material" (she was right) and called the whole thing off, but at least she used her soft, beautiful voice to say goodbye and not the piercing scream.

Another women seduced me with her brilliant mind—she was a Jerry Brown supporter (as was I) but did this complex analysis of the political situation predicting why Jimmy Carter would win in 1976, which proved exactly right. I was dazzled by her intelligence. We spent more time in bed talking than making love, but I enjoyed every minute of it. She eventually got a job in the Middle East with a charitable foundation and left the Bay Area. The composite IQ of the city must have dropped notably when she left San Francisco. While she was moving about in Israel, Jordan, and Egypt, I lost track of her, as there was no email or social media in those days, and I have never found out exactly what happened to her. She just sort of disappeared. In retrospect, I now think she might have been a CIA recruit, as she was exactly the kind of brilliant analyst they might have wanted. Who knows?

In retrospect, it was dangerous having so many lovers and taking a chance on losing my true love, Judy, but at the time, I was addicted to all the excitement, and it was fun, fun, fun.

In addition to all the fun times, I had some embarrassing episodes. Gays and lesbians were starting to come out en masse, and many had migrated to the Bay Area but still weren't totally sure of their sexuality. For a few months, I became something of a magnet for soon-to-be lesbians. My first two semiserious relationships were both with women who were on the fence in terms of sexual orientation.

I didn't understand homosexuality. It was a foreign concept to me. I wasn't gay and had not yet known enough "out" gays to ascertain which people might be. I did lots of stupid things. For example, when I was having trouble in my relationship with Karen, I asked her "friend" Martha for some tips, never imagining that Karen might be a closet lesbian and that Martha was my main competition for Karen's affections. Martha gave me lots of wonderful tips, all designed to undermine me, and I was too naïve to realize it. After sleeping with me for three months, Karen dumped me and moved in with Martha. You would think I'd learn. No.

Within a few weeks, I was involved with another attractive woman, Connie. We had great sex for two months, but I never felt a real emotional connection with her. When I mentioned it, she admitted she thought she might be a lesbian.

"Were you faking all those orgasms?" I asked.

"No, but I was fantasizing about a woman much of the time," she said. Great.

Connie and I remained close allies at work, but we went separate directions for sex.

One of my dubious ideas for a book led to another embarrassing encounter. It was the only time in my life I paid for sex. I had this half-baked idea about a writing a book on the best massage parlors of the Bay Area, so I visited one of the best-known parlors in Berkeley to learn how they worked. I was greeted by a lovely redhead, probably in her early twenties, who introduced me to a half dozen other sexy young women and told me to take my pick. I chose the greeter, since we had chatted a little already, and I felt more comfortable with her. When I asked her name, she said, "My working name is Bambi, but you can call me anything you want." I called her Bambi for lack of anything more creative springing to mind. "Red" was too obvious.

We went to a room with a bed and a partial bath (sink and stool, no shower). We got the financial business out of the way, and I paid her in cash. I wasn't totally naïve and had left my wallet, credit cards, and such at home.

She removed all her clothes—she was only wearing skimpy, see-through lingerie to begin with—and helped me remove mine. She led me to a large shower room where we had a delightful shower together. We returned to the bedroom, did our "massage" business, and chatted pleasantly for a time. She used the sink to wash me off, dried me with a big, fluffy towel, and helped me get dressed. She gave me a card with her name and hours of work and suggested that I visit her again soon. I left the parlor and walked a block to a coffee shop for something to drink. When I paid for my coffee, I fully understood how the parlors worked.

Most of my cash was missing. I had gone to the parlor with $200 in cash. I had paid her $90 (this was the mid-1970s), but now I only had $30. Someone had helped themselves to another $80. I had been had. I could complain (to the police? the parlor management?) but had no proof. Bambi was with me every second I was in the parlor, so clearly she didn't steal my money, but just as clearly, someone must have come into the room while we were showering (probably the whole point of the long shower in the adjoining room) and took most of my cash—leaving enough that my clip wasn't too obviously empty to require closer examination, something unlikely to happen as long as a naked woman was guiding me about the place. I learned my lesson and never went to a pay-to-lay place again. I dropped the idea for the book, as I could see that I would go broke getting ripped off as I made the rounds of the dozens of parlors in the Bay Area. Another best seller down the drain.

I did managed to work Bambi and this experience into other books over the years. Be careful around writers. You'll end up in their books.

Soon I was exploring another dubious idea. In the 1970s in California, there seemed to be a swing club on every other block. One of my lovers wanted to try the sex clubs, and I decided it would make a great article for a local paper—the best sex clubs in the San Francisco Bay Area. However, after hitting a half dozen clubs, I got bored with the scene. It wasn't that I was jealous of my partner being with other men and women.

The clubs made me better understand the famous line from George Orwell's classic *1984* in which Winston tells Julia that he loves her freedom as well as her body. I later read that the artist Salvador Dali said a similar thing about his lover, Gala.

What turned me off about the clubs was the lack of any real connection beyond the purely physical. I was always more a romantic than a pure sensualist. Decades later, this would be called "the girlfriend experience" (one TV version starred Elvis Presley's granddaughter) to distinguish it from the casual sex one might have at a sex club, with a prostitute, or even a pickup at the bar for a one-night stand. There wasn't much new to write about the purely physical act of sex over and over when it had no emotional element.

Plus, to be honest, many of the people at the clubs were less than attractive, and while you were not required to have sex with anyone in particular, declining too many invitations was considered rude.

Around this time, I had started writing what I considered my "writers' trilogy"—three books in which the main characters were all writers, although each book had different characters.

The first was *The Truly Enlightened Don't Write Books*, which I thought was a clever title. It was about five writers and how their lives intertwined over several decades. It featured the cliché of a prostitute with a heart of gold who saved the main character, temporarily, before he died. It had some wonderful passages mixed with some bizarre and poorly designed plot loops that required a couple of literal "miracles" to reach a semilogical ending. It has been said that a novel should make readers laugh (or at least smile), cry (or at least tear up), or both. I think my novel indirectly achieved both by having plots so convoluted that the few people to read them laughed until they cried.

Seriously (humor being our best defense against insanity and depression), *The Truly Enlightened Don't Write Books* ended with the death of the main character. According to their reports, it did make my readers cry (all six of them). The title caught the attention of a handful of editors, and it was read, but everyone hated it. Strike one.

The second manuscript in my never-to-be-published trilogy was titled *Would You Like to Be a Character in My Next Novel?* It was an expanded version of a personal ad I had written for the *San Francisco Bay Guardian*. Personal ads were becoming a phenomenon around that time, and the *Guardian* had one of the best sections in the Bay Area. I was spending much of my day writing, the pickup scene at bars was never my thing, and the situation in the office was getting too complicated with half a dozen ex-lovers and part-time lovers circling around me. I decided to explore a new way to meet women. The personals were a boon. I wrote a series of great personal ads, met dozens of women, and enjoyed intimate relations with several of them. This was so successful that I built a novel around the concept. While the ads were successful, the novel was once more a total bust. The title got me in the door at a few publishing houses, but the novel wasn't good and was repeatedly rejected, often in insulting ways. "Do you have any idea how women actually think?" "This is too depressing to be a comedy and too flippant to be a tragedy." Strike two.

The third manuscript, *Writers, Lovers, and Other Fools*, consisted of a series of short stories and nonfiction pieces about writers and writing. Again, the title was catchy enough (along with my clever query letters) to get the manuscript read by five or six editors, but once more, everyone rejected it. Strike three.

I was running out of ideas. I was running out of energy. I was running out of confidence in my writing (after about a thousand people have told you that you can't write, you start to wonder if they might be right). I was running out of confidence in my sex life. How many more women could I turn into lesbians before I started to question my lovemaking techniques? Seriously, there were periods where I was trying to juggle three or four ongoing relationships at a time. It was getting to be exhausting. Then, just as I was considering giving up the playboy lifestyle, I finally stumbled across the California Fantasy Girl of my teenage years.

Wendy was tall, blonde, reminded me of the movie star Carol Lynley, and even drove a sexy red Porsche. When I met her, she had just gotten divorced and said she just wanted to have some fun. We had more than four hundred wild and wonderful nights. Eventually, she was offered a big promotion to a key management job down in San Diego where she had been raised and where her brother, nieces, and parents still lived. It was too good to refuse. She asked me to come along, but I declined as she knew I would. As much fun as we had had, I knew Judy was my soul mate and that my future was with her.

My wild nights with Wendy were over, but we settled into a delightful, long-distance friendship of over forty years until she died of a stroke. It was one of the saddest days of life. I knew I would miss our weekly emails and monthly phone calls and that as I faded into old age in my seventies, I'd miss that there was one less person in the world who remembered me from when I was young and dynamic. But once I had acted out this long-held California fantasy, I was able to move on to other things, including my writing and having a family.

Judy and I continued to see each other once or twice a week during our "separation." She was getting tired of what she termed my "low-down ways" and suggested she might not wait around forever. I realized she was the great love of my life. We began living together again, but beyond that, I didn't have a clue as to what to do next.

Then, the federal government came to my rescue. I saw a job opening in the area of employment law, employee relations, labor relations, and civil rights. It involved being an administrative attorney, someone who did administrative hearings in the federal sector concerning employment disputes and civil rights discrimination cases. The hearings were before administrative judges or arbitrators, not in district court, so one need not be an attorney-at-law to represent the government at the hearings. I applied for such a job and impressed people with my legal writing skills so much that I was offered a position.

It turned out I was good at litigation. At first, they gave me the lemons, cases they expected to lose, so that I could practice on them. I won every one. Soon I was given better cases. I kept winning. I started getting the most important cases, and I kept winning. I would do this job for over three decades, winning hundreds of cases and losing only twice. I never did bother to get my law degree. After the first few years, no one even asked if I had one. I was winning all the major hearings, and everyone assumed I had a law degree. The motto there was "just win, baby!" stolen from Al Davis, owner of the Oakland Raiders football team. No one cared if I had a law degree as long as I won.

Judy was happy, and I was happy. Even the writing started to fall into place. The late 1970s and early 1980s were some of our happiest times. When *Writers, Lovers, and Other Fools* was rejected by book publishers, a couple of editors did note that while a collection of short stories and articles by an unknown author would be impossible to market, some of the stories and articles were good, and I should submit them to magazines and newspapers. I did and managed to sell several of them. These short pieces paid almost nothing (a few hundred dollars at the most, and sometimes I was paid with twenty copies of the magazine), but it gave me some much needed encouragement.

Judy and I worked in downtown San Francisco. The traffic out of the city in evening rush hour was horrific, so we started eating out most weeknights to let the traffic clear before driving home. This was fun but expensive. San Francisco restaurants are not cheap, not the good ones.

I hit upon the idea of how I could make some of these dinners tax deductible. Why not write a book on the restaurants of San Francisco, making the meals a business expense? I wrote a book called *A Romantic's Guide to San Francisco*. It took several months to complete—the subject matter was expanded to include nudist clubs and sex clubs, and the title changed a few times. I had to write at night, my day job now being too hectic to allow for any writing, but I wrote two hours each evening from around ten to midnight, a pattern that I would continue for much of my life. A midnight writer.

The book was published and sold fairly well. I made a few thousand bucks. With this limited success and the articles that I had managed to get published, I found it much easier to get editors to read my new manuscripts.

MUSICAL INTERLUDE:
"California Gurls," Katy Perry
with Snoop Dogg

CHAPTER 10

The Heartbreak Manuscript

———∞∞———

MUSICAL INTERLUDE:
"Nobody Can Take My Dreams from Me,"
John Denver
"Dream On," Aerosmith

I wanted to write something more serious than restaurant and tourist guides, but I thought nonfiction was now the way to go. I wrote a book on Eastern spirituality and sexuality, borrowing much from tantra and the Rajneesh community in Berkeley where I occasionally hung out but never joined.

This manuscript would break my heart twice. The first publisher I sent it to in Seattle called me (calls are almost unheard of at this stage in the process) and went on and on about what a great book it was and how much he wanted it. He begged me to give him a week to make an offer before I signed with some other publisher. I agreed, since none of the twenty-seven other publishers I queried had bothered to reply. I was dubious about getting an offer so quickly, but to my continuing amazement, three days later, I received a FedEx package with a contract offer and a cover letter, again raving about what a remarkable book I had written and how it might change the world.

I went to my literary attorney and had him review the contract. He said it was basically okay but there were a few clauses that should be modified, and he gave me some alternative language. I sent the counteroffer back to the publisher and waited.

And waited. And waited.

Finally, I called to check on the status. "Is there a problem with the changes that my attorney wanted?" I asked.

"No, no. Nothing like that. We still love your book, but we had some loans come due, and we have financing problems, and we may have to file for bankruptcy. I can't sign any new contracts right now, but I definitely want your book. As soon as we clear up these financial issues, I'll get back to you. I promise."

I never heard from him again. A month went by, and I called to get the status. All I got was a voice message saying, "We are sorry, but XYZ Publishing Company has gone out of business."

Great. The one publisher that was dumb enough to think I was a great writer had such poor judgment that his company went bust. Heartbreak number one.

I was about ready to throw my Smith-Corona electric typewriter in the bay and never write another book when I got a letter from Harper & Row's San Francisco division saying they wanted to read my manuscript. I was back on cloud nine. Harper & Row would be so much better than some small publishing company in Seattle even if they had continued to exist. I was practically counting my advance money. Should Judy and I celebrate in Maui or Acapulco?

Harper & Row was a class act. They gave me the name of an editor and a tracking number for my manuscript so I could check on the status from time to time. They warned me upfront that it may take six months to a year before they made a decision.

While I waited, I started writing a new novel. Six months passed, and I called to get the status. "Our editorial board loves it, and we have sent it over to marketing for their review. Can you send us some marketing ideas?"

Marketing? What the heck do I know about marketing?

Months passed. I called again. "We are stuck right now. Our editorial people love it, but our marketing people can't figure out a good way to market it. Give us a little more time, and we'll see what we can do."

"Isn't it the marketing division's job to devise marketing plans?" I asked naively.

"Yes, of course, and they do a great job, but not every book has an obvious target audience. If you have any ideas yourself, please share with us."

I stopped work on the novel and started reading everything I could find about book marketing. I didn't have a clue about marketing. I didn't want to have a clue. I was a writer, not a salesman. Nonetheless, I learned all I could about target audiences, male versus female reading preferences, old versus young, white versus minority, TV ads versus radio, magazine versus newspaper ads, publishing sales reps and bookstore discount terms, etc. I put together a little marketing plan and sent it to Harper & Row.

Another month passed, and I got a nice letter. "With great regret, we have decided not to publish your book. While the editors loved your manuscript, the marketing division felt it was impossible to market at a level to recoup our expenses. We wish you better success with another publisher." I had lost Harper & Row. Heartbreak number two.

Some cynical marketing director at a big publishing company (not Harper & Row) once said, "Any reasonably intelligent person can write a reasonably good book, but what requires real genius is being able to sell the book." He may have been right.

I tried to go back to my novel, but I had lost momentum. The story seemed stupid now. I hated the characters. I hated the plot. I hated the beginning. I was never great at spelling or grammar and had to pay people to copyedit my manuscripts so they were presentable and professional. I had my copyeditor review what I started. She corrected the spelling and grammar, but when I asked her what she thought of the novel so far, she admitted, "I don't understand what it's even about."

In truth, I didn't either. It was a collection of clever phrases that didn't connect in any meaningful way. I threw it away. I was ready to give up writing forever. Who was I fooling? I couldn't write. I could barely spell, and my grammar was atrocious.

That's when new technology came to the rescue or pulled me back into the writing rut, depending upon how one wants to look at it. The personal computer exploded onto the scene. First, I got a word processor in my office to use to write my legal briefs. Then, I bought a PC to write my books at home. With spell-check, grammar check, and all the easy ways to change manuscripts around, I couldn't resist taking another shot at it all, but where to start?

Two publishers (my bankrupt buddy in Seattle and Harper & Row) had liked my little spirituality and sexuality book variously titled *A Sensual Zen, Western Zen*, or *California Zen*. I decided to try self-publishing. Many famous people had done it: Richard Nixon, Mark Twain, Zane Grey, Upton Sinclair, Carl Sandburg, James Joyce, D. H. Lawrence, George Bernard Shaw, Edgar Allen Poe, Henry David Thoreau, and Walt Whitman. Many famous books started by being self-published including *Leaves of Grass, Lady Chatterley's Lover, Ulysses,* and *Common Sense.*

I read *The Self-Publishing Manual* by Dan Poynter. It was a great guide and walked the reader through the process step by step. It took a few months, but I published the book myself. I got some good reviews in the local papers, especially the infamous *Berkeley Barb,* and sold a few hundred copies, but it turned out Harper & Row was right. There was no logical way to market the book.

The *Berkeley Barb*, now long defunct, was always kind to me and did a two-page spread with multiple photos, giving one of my books the best review I ever got. Another bad sign: publishers and magazines and newspapers that liked my stuff all tended to go out of business. Was I ahead of my time or behind my time? More likely the latter.

In any event, self-publishing was not fun. Going to my post office box and finding twenty new orders didn't make me think of all the money I was raking in but of all the time I would have to spend packaging books and preparing mailing labels that night and how I would rather spend that time making love or writing.

I was not interested in being a small businessman or a self-publisher. The sales tax, bookkeeping, code requirements, and all that bunk were a bore. I wanted real publishers to handle the publishing stuff while I wrote, but what could I write that would possibly sell?

Musical Interlude:
"Running on Empty," Jackson Browne

CHAPTER 11

Small Successes, a Big Decision

My lovely wife suggested, "Why don't you write something practical again? The restaurant book did well. You do lots of employment hearings and teach lots of classes on how to avoid civil rights litigation and win the cases when you can't avoid the litigation. Write about that!"

Judy is a perfect wife for a writer. While she does not write herself, she loves to read books. She reads at least a couple of hours a day. She reads all my horrible manuscripts, including the first, second, third, and fifteenth drafts, and she gives me good feedback, mainly things like, "This part here is pretty boring." She's usually right, so when she makes a suggestion, I listen.

I wasn't excited about doing more of what I was already doing on my day job, but it was true that I had learned lots of inside information about employment, civil rights, employee morale, and winning hearings. I took a shot at it, and between how much I knew about the subject and my new PC, the book was easy to write.

I still needed an angle—something to distinguish it from all the other "how to succeed in the workplace" books.

I came up with *Working and Managing in a New Age* and gave it a Zen spin since I was into this anyway. I added a collection of Pot-Shots from one of my favorite cartoonists, Ashleigh Brilliant.

I quickly found a publisher, and the book did well. It got good reviews and was eventually translated into Spanish (and marketed by a firm in Barcelona) and Portuguese (and marketed by a firm in Brazil). Ivy Books, the business division of Random House in New York, picked up the book and did a mass paperback version. I was sent my largest check ever.

I often refer to it as my best-selling book. It wasn't "a" best seller, but it was "my" best seller of all my books. Writers can spin just like politicians.

Having had some modest success with a business/employment book, I tried again with a book titled *Making Work Fun: Doing Business with a Sense of Humor* and again included cartoons from my favorite cartoonists at *The New Yorker*. The book was picked up by Shamrock Press in San Diego. Again, I got some good reviews, including a prepublication endorsement from Ken Blanchard, author of the huge best seller, *The One Minute Manager*. The book sold very well.

Many writers hate the critics, but in general, critics have been kind to me. Most of them ignore my books, but the few who write reviews have always been favorable (or perhaps my publisher sends me only the good ones).

A friend who managed a large organization in Seattle liked *Making Work Fun* so much that he ordered several hundred copies for all of his managers. A hospital in Indiana did the same for its managers.

I even got an agent out of the process surrounding this

book and received my one and only writing award: a modest and nonfinancial award from one of the San Diego libraries that named my book the best new business book of the year. It must have been a slow year for business books, or else my publisher must have been on the selection committee.

I now had four books in print, a scrapbook with more than a dozen favorable reviews, some money in the bank, one little prize, and growing confidence. I began to give serious thought to quitting my day job and writing full time.

I liked my job. I had in effect become a practicing "administrative attorney" ("attorney" meaning a representative in an administrative proceeding as opposed to the term "attorney-at-law," which implied a member of the bar with a law degree) without the bother and expensive of law school. I liked my boss, but my true love was writing.

I was on the verge of giving full-time writing a real shot, when surprise! Judy got pregnant. We had been trying to decide the baby issue for a few years. Did we want a child or not?

We had a good life. We both had well-paying jobs. We had a nice house in the Oakland Hills with a view of San Francisco Bay. The house was surrounded by eucalyptus and pine trees and always had a delightful smell. We traveled to Mexico, Hawaii, Aruba, and Europe and had a trip to China planned. We went skiing at Lake Tahoe. We spent summer weekends on the beach at Sea Ranch. We flew to Vegas to see Frank Sinatra, Elvis, and others in concert. We even drove a Volvo. It was the 1980s, and we were Yuppies. We were in love. We had it all.

Did we want to give up the good life for the dubious joys of parenting? Being political activists, we felt overpopulation was a major problem and weren't sure it was responsible to add to an overcrowded world. We read books such as *The Baby Trap* by Ellen Peck and *The Baby Decision* by Merle Bombardieri.

We even went to a psychologist. The baby question was so big in those days in San Francisco that there were therapists who specialized in helping couples make this monumental decision. After a few sessions, we were still undecided.

Then, we read the single most influential book of our lives: *The Tao of Pooh* by Benjamin Hoff. This cute little book discussed the theory of *wu wei*, going with the flow. We decided to apply this to our lives. Rather than agonizing over the baby decision, we stopped reading books about it, stopped going to therapy, stopped discussing it, stopped making lists of pros and cons, and stopped using birth control. We cast our fate to the wind, and we got hit in the face with another hurricane.

Not literally this time. The first month Judy went off the pill, she got pregnant. We decided it was meant to be: fate, joss, kismet. We were excited and happy. When Judy had amniocentesis done and we learned the baby was a girl, we were ecstatic. We had both wanted a girl. One of the cons of having a child was that we couldn't even select the gender, much less have any control over the child's features or personality. Maybe we were control freaks, but we knew what we wanted and knew having a baby was a random genetic process that gave us no control. Little did we know...

My writing career went on the back burner. This was not the time to take chances and give up a good job. Judy wanted to take a year off after the baby was born, so I would have to be the sole breadwinner, at least temporarily.

The pregnancy went well, and Rhonda was born on September 9, which was Judy's thirty-fifth birthday. What a present! It was the happiest day of our lives.

We had taken Lamaze classes, and I was present for the birth, doing my coaching duties. Rhonda came out screaming and was healthy according to all the tests. I took lots of pictures and sent them to the grandparents in Missouri and New York, who were all delighted. I bought Rhonda her first rose and brought it to her on day two. I couldn't resist writing a special movie-themed baby announcement that we shipped out to all our friends and family around the country.

Garland Productions Proudly Present

A STAR IS BORN

Produced by Judy Garland
Directed by Ron Garland

Introducing and Starring

RHONDA DALE GARLAND

Weight 6 lbs. 7 oz.
Opening in Berkeley, California
September 9, 1984

The Critics Acclaim the New Star:

"Both thumbs up."
Roger Ebert and Gene Siskel, *At the Movies*

"There was some nudity, but it was necessary for the plot and was handled well."
TIME

"We predict round-the-clock showings
will be necessary."
Newsweek

"More action than *Raiders of the Lost Ark*,
more tears than *Terms of Endearment*."
Los Angeles Times

"Rhonda Dale is going to be in a lot
of pictures in the coming years."
San Francisco Chronicle

"Best performance since the first Judy Garland
in the 1954 version of *A Star Is Born*."
The New York Times

"In the future when they say Rhonda,
they won't be thinking of Rhonda Fleming."
Chicago Tribune

The baby announcement was the last thing I would write for months.

CHAPTER 12

Life with Baby Shakes Things Up

Rhonda as never a good sleeper. The first few months were tough. Day-to-day life with a baby was exhausting. I didn't have a spare minute to write.

After six months, Judy was so exhausted that she decided it would be easier to go back to work than take care of a baby all day. She researched daycare and interviewed several prospects. One day, she came home crying, almost hysterical. She couldn't find anyone worthy of our precious little girl, yet she was exhausted from doing it herself all day while I was at work.

We kept looking and finally found a wonderful woman, Mary. She was married to an Iranian Muslim, lived in a big house with a big extended family, and ran a daycare in one large wing of her home. She had a way with kids and cared for only six at a time, assisted by her sister-in-law. Judy went back to work, and our lives became more manageable.

The next three years were happy ones. Rhonda started to sleep a few hours each night, and she was a delight to play with. She learned to walk and talk, and like most parents, we thought each new development was amazing. I recorded everything with hours and hours of video. We took her skiing with us where she played in the snow and said funny things like calling Lake Tahoe "Lake Taco."

I still read a little, but I rarely wrote anything. I missed writing, but there wasn't time.

These were the Reagan years. President Reagan took a hard line against unions and broke the air traffic controllers union. He cut federal jobs, and my section was always understaffed. Our caseload went up because of heavy-handed management, and we went from very busy to overwhelmed, trying to keep up with our motions and hearings. I lost two hearings during the 1980s (my only defeats in more than three decades of litigation) when I didn't have time to properly prepare witnesses.

Reagan was succeeded by Bush (the smart Bush, not the idiot son). Our staff increased, and our workload became realistic again.

Things were going so well that I went to a part-time work schedule so that I had two days a week at home to write. I started a novel based around the idea of reincarnation, but I decided I didn't really believe in reincarnation and lost my passion for the project. I wrote some short stories that didn't sell. I fell back on the tried-and-true and wrote several business/work-related articles that were published in various newspapers and magazines.

Still, I didn't feel like that was "real writing," whatever real writing may be. I wanted to write a novel but didn't have anything new to say.

Once again, Judy came to the rescue with an idea. She said, "Rhonda wants you to tell her a story every night at bedtime, because she likes the stories you make up better than the books you buy to read to her. Maybe you should write those stories down and see if other little kids would like them too."

I did, and so did every other father and mother in the nation who was making up little stories for their kids. The market was saturated with proposed children's books. I have no artistic ability, so I was not able to illustrate my stories like many of the other would-be children's authors could. I was never able to crack this market. It was a completely different set of publishers who didn't know me and didn't care about my limited successes in other publishing fields. I went back to the drawing board or, in this case, a blank computer screen.

Once you starting writing, even if it's crap and doesn't sell, the process alone sometimes fires up the imagination and leads to more ideas. While my children's manuscripts never made it beyond Rhonda's bedtime stories, I was in a mood to write again, so I did a complete about-face and shifted from children's books to porn.

Well, not really. Let's say an "adult" mystery. I had always wanted to write a murder mystery. The genre seemed simple enough with a clear formula, but there were a million such books out there (many of which I enjoyed reading, especially on airplane trips). I knew I needed a unique approach to this genre.

There had been a time, before Rhonda, when Judy and I liked to go to nude beaches, and we joined a naturist club for a few years. Our club, called Lupin, was in the mountains between San Jose and Santa Cruz. Drawing on that experience, I cranked out *Murder at the Nudist Club: A Revealing Mystery*.

The title caught the attention of the editors at the publishing houses. Several asked to read the manuscript, and all of them hated it. In trying to create something radically new, they felt I had created a publishing freak (a book that couldn't be sold because it was too weird). I didn't get form letter rejections for this book. I got two- and three-page rejection letters telling me what a perverted writer I was.

"Mystery fans are conservative, straight-laced people who don't want sex, or if there must be sex to advance the plot, the sex must be off-screen."

"Your work combines a lackluster murder mystery with a series of dull, repetitive sex orgies. It doesn't work as a mystery, and it is even worse as porn."

"You have created the first work of its kind that I can recall: a pornographic murder mystery. I pray it is the last such that I ever have to review."

"I didn't believe this book for a minute. Places like that don't even exist." This letter from a New York City editor who had no clue about the California lifestyle. There were and still are lots of places like that but not in Manhattan, where you'd freeze your ass off if you ran around naked in January. This was a problem I often encountered in dealing with New York editors—they don't understand that there is a world out there west of the Hudson River. I always had better success with California publishers.

More bad reviews:

"Thanks for creating a brand new genre. Now please STOP!"

"I didn't think it possible for a writer to be TOO creative, but I was wrong. We couldn't possibly publish this trash. We would be laughed off the island."

"This sounds like a college boy's sex fantasy, not a serious mystery for adults."

And so forth.

After reading about a dozen of these original, sometimes handwritten, rejection letters, I was longing for the days when I received one-word "Sorry" notes or form letters that always said the same thing: "Not right for our publishing list at this time, but we wish you success elsewhere. Just because a manuscript isn't right for our list does not reflect upon the quality of your work, and it may be better suited for another publisher. We wish you the best and thank you for thinking of us" or some gobbledygook to that effect.

While I was waiting for *Murder at the Nudist Club* to make me a superstar, I started another book in the same ill-fated vein. *Who Is Killing the Great Lovers of San Francisco?* was based on the concept that *Playgirl* did an article on the most handsome single guys in the Bay Area, and they started getting murdered one by one by...who? Was it a murderous female who had slept with all of them but failed to marry any of these rich and attractive young men or an envious male rival who was upset at being left off the *Playgirl* list?

Well, we will never know. Long before I finished the book and decided which of my many suspects would be the actual killer, the feedback I got for *Murder at the Nudist Club* was so bad that I decided to put the book on the back burner where it eventually died along with all the great lovers of San Francisco. Yet another unsolved crime in the City by the Bay. Not up there with the Zodiac Killer but close.

I moved on to a nonfiction book on the survival of the humanity. The first version was called *Children of the Future Age*, a title taken from the William Blake poem, "A Little Girl Lost."

> Children of the future age
> Reading this indignant page
> Know that in a former time
> Love, sweet love, was thought a crime

However, before I got very far, I had to worry about my own survival. It was October 1989, and the Bay Area was abuzz with the first Bay Bridge World Series between the San Francisco Giants and the Oakland A's. Judy and I left work early to pick up Rhonda at daycare to be home for the start of the game. At age five, Rhonda was a big Jose Canseco fan, and even she was excited about the World Series.

We reached the daycare facility, and Rhonda was putting on her sweater when I found myself down on the floor like someone had pulled a rug out from under me. For half a second, I thought I had started to pass out and had fallen, and my hand went instinctively toward my heart as if it was a heart attack, but then I noticed everyone else on the ground too. I heard rumbling and saw the furniture dancing around the floor.

"Quick, everyone outside!" We grabbed the kids and rushed, as best we could with the ground shaking like crazy under our feet, out into the open yard where nothing smaller than a tree was going to be able to fall on us.

Soon the shaking was over. We sat in the yard in for a while and laughed about our little scare. The kids were running around having fun. This was California. We were all used to earthquakes. More parents arrived to pick up their kids. "Did you feel that one?" we asked. "No, I was driving and didn't notice anything." We moved on to discussing baseball, and the earthquake was forgotten for a few minutes.

When we got to the car, I turned on the radio to the pregame show and found my reception was nil. I tried all the buttons and couldn't get anything. "Earthquake must have loosened a wire in my radio," I said.

I started to drive home. A few miles later at the freeway entrance, I noticed a small problem: the freeway ramp was gone. We understood this quake was not just another one of our little rumbles. Still, we didn't understand how bad it was.

We managed to weave through city streets. At a stoplight, I noticed the guy next to me punching his radio buttons with great annoyance. I rolled my window down. "Is your radio dead too?" I said.

"Yeah, damn thing just went out completely. I was listening to the pregame show."

"Think it could be the earthquake?" I asked, still thinking something was wrong with our individual car radios and not thinking that every radio station in the area had been knocked off the air.

"Could be," he said.

All the traffic lights went dead, and the traffic jam got worse. After a few minutes of gridlock, I got out of my car and walked up the street to where several people were standing. "Anyone know how bad this is?"

"Yeah, it's bad. Real bad. One of the radio stations came back up on emergency power. Freeways have collapsed all over Oakland and Berkeley. The Bay Bridge has collapsed. The Marina district in San Francisco is on fire. The World Series has been canceled. The stadium is being evacuated. This was the Big One."

Well, it turned out it wasn't the Big One, but it was pretty damn big. We got home to find our house still hanging on the hillside but barely. Many other houses weren't so lucky.

The quake terrified Rhonda. She didn't sleep well again for months. We had structural engineers examine our house and were assured that the next quake would send our lovely redwood dwelling down the hill into Shepherd Canyon. We had to spend thousands of dollars to retrofit the house, and still no one would guarantee its stability.

Try sleeping in a house that you know may collapse and fall into a canyon at any moment without warning. Try doing it when you are five years old.

There was no way to downplay the danger. Earthquake news dominated the newspaper, TV, radio, and daycare center discussions for weeks. Rhonda would be starting kindergarten next year, and the school (Montclair) sat directly on the Hayward fault. If the quake didn't get her at home, it would get her at school.

Judy and Rhonda became desperate to move, but with the collapse of the freeways came the collapse of the Bay Area real estate market. We were stuck—the Year of Living Dangerously.

The bad news kept on coming. Over the next year, Judy started to lose control of her hands, making it impossible to use the computer and continue to work. She was eventually diagnosed with multiple sclerosis and had to quit her job.

We had wanted to get away from our house before it collapsed and get Rhonda to a different school that wasn't directly over a fault line, but now things were even more complicated. With only one salary and the value of our house cut in half after the 1989 quake, there wasn't much we could afford in a good school district in the Bay Area.

Our house had been on the market for many months with no takers and few lookers when one day a woman from Taiwan showed up with her agent to say our house was perfect. Perfect? Yes, she was into feng shui. Our house faced the right direction, our front door faced the right direction, and our house was in balance (spiritually, not structurally). We had to disclose the earthquake issues and our retrofitting, but she didn't care about any of that. "I've lived in Taiwan, earthquake country, most of my life. I'm not worried about earthquakes. The positive forces will protect me," she said. (Turns out she was right. She lived there for twenty years before she sold it and moved on, and there was never any damage from future quakes.)

The lady from Taiwan made us a straight cash offer. She was serious. Now we needed to move ourselves, somewhere and quickly. We were looking at houses about sixty miles out of the city in Fairfield, and I was dreading the long commute when unexpectedly I got offered a job in St. Louis, Missouri.

Getting job offers out of the blue wasn't anything new for me. Because I had a good reputation as someone who won 99 percent of his hearings, many people wanted to hire me. Most often the job offers were in Washington, DC, or Los Angeles, and we had no desire to live in either place, even before Judy became disabled. With Judy not working, we weren't interested in another expensive city like Washington.

The St. Louis offer was intriguing. St. Louis was a low-cost area, and my family (Rhonda's grandparents, aunts, uncles and cousins) all lived in Missouri. I flew to St. Louis for a final interview to meet my would-be boss, and he turned out to be a great guy. He had read some of my articles, thought I was just what his office needed, and offered me a job on the spot. It seemed like the perfect arrangement at the perfect time.

We moved to St. Louis in the summer of 1991. As we drove across the Missouri River into St. Louis County, we all sang "Meet Me in St. Louis" along with a cassette recording of the original Judy Garland.

CHAPTER 13

The St. Louis Blues

Everything has pros and cons. We had a great house in a safe area with good schools. The job turned out to be what I expected, and my boss was a great guy. My extended family was in the area.

This was a major plus. I have a great family. My maternal grandmother was still alive, and she was a saint, although fading into Alzheimer's disease in her mid-eighties. Even when she lost it and didn't know who we all were, she was still amazingly pleasant and said things like, "I don't know who you are, but I know you are someone I love, and I'm glad you've come to visit me."

My parents were wonderful people and lived about one hundred miles away near Cape Girardeau, so Rhonda could see her grandparents regularly and for all major holidays. My aunts, uncles, and cousins were all great people. Most families have at least one bad apple, but everyone in my family was fantastic. If we had a bad apple, it would have been me. Writers will happen in the best of families. An occasional mutation can't be helped.

There were lots of pluses to the move, but there were also cons. After twenty years in New York and California, St.

Louis was a cultural shock. It was conservative, puritanical, and provincial. We compounded our problem by buying a house in an especially conservative area, Chesterfield. We lived three houses over from Jim Talent, the local right-wing congressman, who in a few years would serve a brief term in the United States Senate where he was a darling of the lunatic fringe religious right. Most of our neighbors, while decent people, were almost as right-wing as he was.

When we lived in the Bay Area, we were considered (and considered ourselves) moderates. Moderate, of course, compared to people in San Francisco, Berkeley, and Oakland. In St. Louis, we were seen as extreme leftists.

We chose Chesterfield because my cousin Craig (about four years younger than me and a banker) lived in that area and had two delightful girls, one older and one younger than Rhonda. Initially, being near family offset having the narrow-minded neighbors, but we had lived there only six months when Craig's bank was taken over in a merger, and he was transferred to the Wells Fargo in Minneapolis. We lost the main reason to be in that far western suburb.

We had a lot of trouble finding liberal friends. Finally, in desperation, we turned to God.

We rarely attended church over the years as we were more inclined toward Eastern spirituality, Buddhism, and Zen. Even a few flakes like Bhagwan Shree Rajneesh, who taught a beautiful philosophy and failed to live up to it, proving hypocrisy isn't limited to Western, monotheistic religions. When we had attended church, it was of the New Age, New Thought Christianity, positive thinking variety.

We realized we needed a liberal religion to find liberal friends. I started making the rounds every Sunday morning, trying out one church after another—everything from the

United Church of Christ to several congregations of Unitarians. We found Unitarian Universalism, with its lack of creed and create-your-own-theology approach, well suited to us. It let us pick and choose ideas we liked from lots of different religions, East and West. We joined the church. In years to come, I was a Sunday school teacher for four years and became the chair of the Sunday school committee.

My despair at the cultural gap in St. Louis and our quest to find a liberal community gave me an idea for a book titled *Slightly to the Left of St. Louis: A Guide for the Progressive Newcomer*. The book covered everything from neighborhoods (we later found several progressive communities in the St. Louis area and ended up moving away from the outer burbs of Chesterfield) to churches, nudist clubs (yes, there was one), sex clubs, strip clubs (the research was exhausting, but someone had to do it, and I wanted my book to be accurate), romantic restaurants, and the liberal media like the *Riverfront Times*.

It was an easy book to write—a list of progressive and alternative lifestyle activities in St. Louis isn't that long. It was an effort to pump it up to one hundred pages, and much of that consisted of listings of restaurants that were "progressive" in the sense of being something other than a steak house such as a Thai or Vietnamese restaurant. While easy to write, it was impossible to publish. The progressive market in St. Louis could have held a convention in an SUV if any of us had been misguided enough to have driven such a vehicle. (Years later, much to my regret, I had to get an SUV for my wife's wheelchair.)

The lack of publishers led to yet another idea: e-books. The technology was changing almost monthly. Suddenly, it was possible to create an electronic book on a personal computer and sell it online through various websites, including one's own.

I was eager to explore the new technology, and this was the perfect book for it. E-books had many advantages. They were cheap to produce, costing essentially nothing. You could add color, animation, music, videos, and all kinds of bells and whistles that you couldn't add to a traditional paper book. You didn't have to wrap and package the material and mail it to someone. You sent it to them as an email attachment.

Slightly to the Left of St. Louis turned out to be relatively easy to sell. The market was just local. There were only a handful of places worth running ads, and the internet provided lots of options for marketing.

An administrator at St. Louis Community College bought the e-book, loved it, and sent me an email asking if I'd like to teach a class on writing and publishing at the Meramec campus.

I had always enjoyed teaching (and did lots of training on my day job), so I jumped at the opportunity. I began a part-time career and taught writing and publishing classes at the St. Louis Community College for more than ten years.

I collect quotes on many topics, especially writing. When I taught my writing class at the community college, I used them as discussion topics. Here are a few examples.

> "I write because I want to change the world."
> —Alvin Toffler

> "To hold a pen is to be a war."
> —Voltaire

"Few novelists play golf, go bowling, or watch much television. Novel writing is like heroin addiction: it takes all you've got."

—James N. Frey

"Every asshole in the world wants to write."

—Judith Rossner

"The act of writing is an act of optimism. You would not take the trouble to do it if you felt that it didn't matter."

—Edward Albee

"The first draft of anything is shit."

—Ernest Hemingway

"Money to a writer is time to write."

—Frank Herbert

"Even if I could not earn a penny from my writing, I would earn my livelihood at something else and continue to write at night."

—Irving Wallace

I also cited a few inspirational examples to encourage my students not to give up in the face of adversity. Easier said than done, as I myself have given up periodically, but each time I eventually tried again.

Dr. Seuss's first children's book was rejected by twenty-seven publishers. The twenty-eighth, Vanguard Press, sold six million copies.

Louis L'Amour received 350 rejections before he made his first sale. He went on to sell more than two hundred million copies of his Western novels.

Margaret Mitchell's classic *Gone with the Wind* was turned down by more than twenty-five publishers.

John Grisham's first novel was rejected by fifteen publishers and thirty agents before it went on to sell more than sixty million copies.

Jack London received six hundred rejection slips before he sold his first story.

There are hundreds of stories like this of repeated rejection turning into fabulous successes. Of course, there are probably millions of stories where the rejections go on forever, and we never hear about them at all. Perhaps like me, the authors finally get a few books published, but none become best sellers, so they are still largely unknown.

Although I enjoyed teaching and met lots of interesting people, after ten years, I gave it up for three reasons. It was taking time away from my writing (as my life got more complicated over the years, writing time was becoming more precious). My classes were always full (word got around that it was an informative and fun class), and there were always conflicts about class size. Some people would show up even after being told the class was full, try to crash the class, and beg me to let them stay. If I let them, I got in trouble with the college, and if I didn't, the student became upset and thought I was a jerk. Plus, it grew to be depressing in an indirect way.

Everyone in the class had hopes of becoming a published writer, yet over the ten years I taught, only a tiny percentage of the students got anything published. Their dreams were often crushed. Although I started every new semester with a warning about how difficult it was to get anything published and suggested alternatives like self-publishing and e-books, both of which I had done myself, virtually all the students felt that they would be the exception, that they would get published by a major New York house. Maybe one in fifty would do so, and even then, it would almost always be nonfiction—diet books, business books, skeet-shooting books, medical books, even an airplane repair book called *Cessnas for Dummies* or something to that effect. It was rarely what they wanted to write such as poetry or novels.

The people in the class were almost all interesting and intelligent, yet the deck was stacked against them, and 95 percent would fail to publish anything. I kept in touch with hundreds of students over the years via email, and it depressed me to see them repeatedly rejected by publishers and agents and become so dejected.

I felt the very existence of my class was giving people false hope. This, combined with the time and enrollment issues, caused me to give up teaching at the community college after a decade.

CHAPTER 14

The E-Book Era

My marginal success with *Slightly to the Left of St. Louis* encouraged me to try more e-books.

I still had my unpublished manuscript, *Murder at the Nudist Club*, gathering dust, and it was easy to convert the Word document into an e-book and run some ads. The book started selling. While the editors had hated it with a passion, the kinky people I found on the internet thought it was brilliant or at least good enough that no one asked for their money back.

Several readers emailed me and asked if I had other books available.

I spun the reading list for the class I taught at the community college into an e-book titled *Reading to Write: 50 Books Every Aspiring Writer Should Read*. Here are some of the books I discussed and recommended.

- *The Art of Fiction*, John Gardner
- *The Aristos*, John Fowles
- *The Book of Laughter and Forgetting*, Milan Kundera

- *The Brothers Karamazov*, Fyodor Dostoyevsky
- *Cat's Cradle*, Kurt Vonnegut
- *The Catcher in the Rye*, J. D. Salinger
- *Chop Wood, Carry Water*, Rick Fields
- *A Confession*, Leo Tolstoy
- *Creation*, Gore Vidal
- *Dune*, Frank Herbert
- *The End of the Affair*, Graham Greene
- *Fates Worse Than Death*, Kurt Vonnegut
- *For Whom the Bell Tolls*, Ernest Hemingway
- *The French Lieutenant's Woman*, John Fowles
- *The Golden Notebook*, Doris Lessing
- *How to Read a Book*, Mortimer J. Adler and Charles Van Doren
- *If You Want to Write*, Brenda Ueland
- *Immortality*, Milan Kundera
- *Kalki*, Gore Vidal
- *A Lifetime Reading Plan*, Clifton Fadiman
- *Man's Fate*, André Malraux
- *Of Human Bondage*, W. Somerset Maugham
- *On Becoming a Novelist*, John Gardner
- *On Writing Well*, William Zinsser

- *Palm Sunday*, Kurt Vonnegut
- *The Picture of Dorian Gray*, Oscar Wilde
- *Point Counter Point*, Aldous Huxley
- *The Portable Voltaire*
- *Reader's Encyclopedia*, William Rose Benet
- *A Religion of Realities*, Kenneth L. Patton
- *The Satanic Verses*, Salman Rushdie
- *The Self-Publishing Manual*, Dan Poynter
- *The Sirens of Titan*, Kurt Vonnegut
- *Starting from Scratch*, Rita Mae Brown
- *The Summing Up*, W. Somerset Maugham
- *The Unbearable Lightness of Being*, Milan Kundera
- *The Women's Room*, Marilyn French
- *A Writer's Notebook*, W. Somerset Maugham
- *Writers on Writing*, compiled by Jon Winokur
- *Writing Down the Bones*, Natalie Goldberg
- *Writing to Learn*, William Zinsser

My e-book was published in the 1990s. Since then I have discovered several additional books that I would recommend in a current version.

- *13 Ways of Looking at the Novel*, Jane Smiley. This

book is a must read for anyone who writes novels.

- *How I Became a Famous Novelist*, Steve Hely
- *How to Become a Famous Writer Before You're Dead*, Ariel Gore. These two books are similar with good tips and good fun. From Gore, my favorite funny line is "Sometimes it seems like a writer has to put on a monkey suit to get any attention."
- *Inventing the Truth: The Art and Craft of Memoir*, William Zinsser. A collection of great articles from the likes of Henry Louis Gates, Jr. and Toni Morrison on writing memoirs and autobiographies and the difference between the two.
- *A Long Way Down*, Nick Hornby. A sad and funny book about a group of suicidal people who decide to start a book group that reads only books by authors who have killed themselves, and there are lots of such authors from which to choose. Suicide is a major occupational hazard of writers.
- *Negotiating with the Dead: A Writer on Writing*, Margaret Atwood. Her novels are brilliant, so as you might expect, her book on writing is brilliant.
- *On Writing: A Memoir of the Craft*, Stephen King. Another author who knows a thing or two about writing and is willing to share. Great book.
- *Portrait of an Artist, as an Old Man*, Joseph Heller. I discovered this book in a weird way. I was playing around with different titles for my own book, and this was one that I considered briefly. I rejected it

because I thought calling myself an "artist" was too pretentious given my limited successes, and when I searched for the title on Amazon.com, I found that someone had already used it. So I had to read it, and it turned out be excellent.

- *The Shadow of the Wind*, Carlos Ruiz Zafon. This novel introduced the concept of the "cemetery of forgotten books." I fear this is where all my books will go.
- *Death of a Writer*, Michael Collins. A murder mystery but so much more.
- *Making a Literary Life: Advice for Writers and Other Dreamers*, Carolyn See. My favorite line is "I'd like to be remembered, by at least a few people, for at least a little while." Between this insightful book and her novels, I think she will achieve this goal.
- *Reader's Block*, David Markson. Written in a seemingly random sequence of short paragraphs and a style that I would normally find annoying, I found it brilliant.
- *The Savage Detectives*, Roberto Bolaño. This is the book that gave me the idea to write my autobiography. Discussed in more detail elsewhere.
- *Why I Write: Thoughts on the Craft of Fiction*, Will Blythe, editor. A collection of articles by famous writers on why they write.
- *A Writer's San Francisco: A Guided Journey for the Creative Soul*, Eric Maisel. While the focus is on one city, the truths are universal.

- *The Written World: The Power of Stories to Shape People, History, Civilization*, Martin Puchner. This history of books and writing will remind you why books are so vital to civilization.

Reading to Write sold well over the internet and was easy to market to writers' groups and organizations. Later, I revised it, expanded it, changed the title and emphasis, and put out another e-book called *Reading to Think: A Thought-Provoking Guide to Over 100 of the Most Thought-Provoking Books in the World*. In addition to the books in *Reading to Write*, I added the following.

- *After Many a Summer Dies the Swan*, Aldous Huxley
- *Anais Nin Reader*
- *The Aquarian Conspiracy*, Marilyn Ferguson
- *The Art of Loving*, Erich Fromm
- *The Awakening*, Kate Chopin
- *Being Liberal in an Illiberal Age*, Jack Mendelsohn
- *Beyond Freedom and Dignity*, B. F. Skinner
- *Beyond Good and Evil*, Friedrich Nietzsche
- *The Book of the Secrets*, Bhagwan Shree Rajneesh
- *A Brief History of Time*, Stephen Hawking
- *The Chemistry of Love*, Michael Liebowitz
- *Civilization and Its Discontents*, Sigmund Freud

- *Civilized Couple's Guide to Extramarital Adventure*, Albert Ellis
- *Cosmic Trigger*, Anton Wilson
- *The Crack in the Cosmic Egg*, Joseph Chilton Pearce
- *The Denial of Death*, Ernest Becker
- *The Dragons of Eden*, Carl Sagan
- *Eros and Civilization*, Herbert Marcuse
- *Essays and Aphorisms*, Arthur Schopenhauer
- *The Ethics of Ambiguity*, Simone De Beauvoir
- *Exuberance: A Philosophy of Happiness*, Paul Kurtz
- *Existential Sexuality*, Peter Koestenbaum
- *The Expanding Circle: Ethics and Sociobiology*, Peter Singer
- *Go Tell It on the Mountain*, James Baldwin
- *God, Power, and Evil*, David Ray Griffin
- *The Grapes of Wrath*, John Steinbeck
- *Handbook to Higher Consciousness*, Ken Keyes
- *The Heart of the Matter*, Graham Greene
- *How to Think about God*, Mortimer Adler
- *The Iceman Cometh*, Eugene O'Neill
- *The Illusion of Immortality*, Corliss Lamont
- *Illusions*, Richard Bach

- *The Immortalist*, Alan Harrington
- *Ingersoll the Magnificent*, Joseph Lewis
- *Invisible Man*, Ralph Ellison
- *Island*, Aldous Huxley
- *Leaves of Grass*, Walt Whitman
- *Life After Life*, Raymond Moody
- *Life Against Death*, Norman Brown
- *Looking Backward*, Edward Bellamy
- *Love and Will*, Rollo May
- *Love Me Tomorrow*, Robert Rimmer
- *Man into Superman*, Robert Ettinger
- *Marriage and Morals*, Bertrand Russell
- *Meditations*, Marcus Aurelius
- *The Medium, the Mystic, and the Physicist*, Lawrence LeShan
- *Mind and Nature*, Gregory Bateson
- *Montaigne's Essays*
- *The Myth of Sisyphus*, Albert Camus
- *The Nature of Things*, Lucretius
- *A New Look at Love*, Elaine Hatfield and William Walster
- *1984*, George Orwell

- *The Occult*, Colin Wilson
- *Old Goriot*, Honoré de Balzac
- *Overcoming the Fear of Death*, David Gordon
- *Pensées*, Blaise Pascal
- *The Phenomenon of Man*, Pierre Teilhard de Chardin
- *The Philosophy of Humanism*, Corliss Lamont
- *The Physics of Immortality*, Frank Tipler
- *The Plague*, Albert Camus
- *Planethood*, Ferencz/Keyes
- *The Prospect of Immortality*, Robert Ettinger
- *The Rapids of Change*, Robert Theobald
- *Reincarnation: The Phoenix Fire Mystery*, Head/Cranston
- *A Religion of Realities: A Philosophy of Religion*, Kenneth Patton
- *The Road Less Traveled*, M. Scott Peck
- *Science and the Modern World*, Colin Whitehead
- *The Seven Mysteries of Life*, Guy Murchie
- *Sex Diary of a Metaphysician*, Colin Wilson
- *Sex in History*, Reay Tannahill
- *The Souls of Black Folk*, W. E. B. Du Bois
- *Stalking the Wild Pendulum*, Itzhak Bentov

- *The Story of Philosophy*, Will Durant
- *Stranger in a Strange Land*, Robert A. Heinlein
- *The Tao of Physics*, Fritjof Capra
- *The Universe is a Green Dragon*, Brian Swimme
- *Up-Wingers*, F. M. Esfandiary
- *The Varieties of Religious Experience*, William James
- *The Virtue of Selfishness*, Ayn Rand
- *Walden*, Henry David Thoreau
- *War and Peace*, Leo Tolstoy
- *Who Dies?* Stephen and Ondrea Levine
- *Why I'm Not a Christian*, Bertrand Russell
- *Why Men Rule*, Steven Goldberg
- *Without Marx or Jesus*, Jean-Francois Revel
- *The Wisdom of Insecurity*, Alan Watts
- *Your God Is Too Small*, J. B. Phillips

Twenty years later, if I were doing this book today, I would recommend a few of my favorites that I have since read.

- *American Nations*, Colin Woodard. The author argues that America has never been a single united nation but eleven different regional cultures that have managed to coexist.

- *Being Nobody, Going Nowhere: Meditations on the Buddhist Path*, Ayya Khema. This book was published in 1987, but I didn't discover it until years later. By that time, I had read so many books on Eastern religions that it took a lot to impress me. Hers did.
- *The Dark Side*, Alan R. Pratt. A massive collection of quotes and articles from ancient Greece to the present on the futility of life. Don't read this if you are already suicidal, but I loved it, as it fits with my approach in *Humanity Sucks*.
- *In One Person*, John Irving. I enjoyed many of his earlier books, but this one blew me away. I had dreams about it. Among the thousands of items I underlined while reading this, one sentence had the character, an obsessive reader, note that if he ever found the love of his life it would have to be someone who was also a reader. I fully understand this. I cannot imagine marrying or living with anyone who didn't share my love of books.
- *A People's History of the United States*, Howard Zinn. A different version of history than we were taught in grade school, high school, or college. You may not agree with it all. I don't, but it will help you understand how the United States went from our alleged glorious founding fathers to a buffoon like Donald Trump.
- *The Power*, Naomi Alderman. I read this novel because President Obama listed it as one of his favorites of 2017. It is a fascinating story about how everything changes when women become more

physically powerful than men. There is a disease called gynophobia, the fear of women. It is already one of the most dangerous illnesses in the world and infects every religion and culture. Imagine how much more frightening women could be if they were not only more sexually powerful but physically more lethal as well.

- *Sapiens: A Brief History of Humankind*, Yuval Noah Harari. This is another wonderful book that helps explain how humans came to be the paradox we are: partly good, partly bad. He wrote an excellent sequel that looks into the far future titled *Homo Deus*.

- *Submission*, Michel Houellebecq. A novel about the Islamic takeover of France and a critique of French literature, it reminded me that a writer can be famous in one country and unknown in most of the rest of the world.

- *This Other Eden*, Ben Elton. A fun novel about a serious subject—the ecological collapse of planet earth and competing alternatives for dealing with it.

- *Our Final Invention: Artificial Intelligence and the End of the Human Era*, James Barrat. I discovered this book when Elon Musk listed it as one of his favorites. Barrat states, "Someday soon, perhaps within your lifetime, some group or individual will create human-level AI, commonly called AGI. Shortly after that, someone (or some thing) will create an AI that is smarter than humans." Barrat is very worried that this may be the end of humankind, but as I have grown pessimistic about rapid biological evolution, I see AI as potentially hopeful, perhaps as an augmentation.

I could go on and on with great books that I've read in the last twenty years, but then this would become a sequel to *Reading to Think*, and I'd never get back to my own little story.

Reading to Think sold okay but not as well as *Reading to Write*. There are more people who want to write than think, I guess.

Still, you can't lose money on an e-book. It's all profit. I continued with this approach. Since I had become a Unitarian Universalist, I was excited about discovering this "little-known" group that claims five presidents and other famous members including Ben Franklin, Thomas Jefferson, John Adams, Adlai Stevenson, Frank Lloyd Wright, and Beatrice Potter.

I wrote a book called *The Joys of Unitarian Universalism: Religion for People Who Think*. (I've always been big on thinking.) I should have thought some more before writing it. Apparently, most people interested in religion aren't all that interested in thinking. The book didn't make much money, and I began to sour on the whole e-book idea. I felt I had exhausted that specialized market and didn't have any more good ideas for e-books. It was time to return to fiction and try another novel, but what?

MUSICAL INTERLUDE:
"Have All the Songs Been Written?"
The Killers

CHAPTER 15

The Power of Anger

―⚬⚬⚬―

*"I write to convey my anger at all that
I think is wrong in this world."*

—NORMAN MAILER,
"At the Point of My Pen"

In 1995, the United States was transfixed by the O. J. Simpson murder trial. Since litigation was my main source of income, I followed the trial in a half-hearted way. It was clear to me that Simpson was guilty, and I assumed he would be convicted despite all the clever tactics his superstar defense team employed. It was shocking and disappointing when the jury found him not guilty. What the hell were these people thinking?

Emotions had won out over reason, and the jury (mostly African American) had chosen to stick it to the man (the establishment, the police, the court system) rather than pursue justice.

The verdict destroyed more of the limited faith I had left in the human race. I had always been an advocate of civil rights. I had marched in civil rights marches in the 1960s. I had worked in the area of civil rights most of my adult life, yet here, when minorities had some power (the power of the jury box), they had acted as irrationally as white people had for centuries.

It didn't seem to matter what race you were. Give someone power, and they will abuse it. The entire human race seemed bigoted, irrational, cruel, and downright stupid. Everyone seemed to dislike everyone who wasn't just like them.

I had been a child of the 1960s who wanted to create a new world with peace and justice for all. There had been many setbacks and disillusionments over the years: the assassinations of Dr. King and Bobby Kennedy, the presidencies of Nixon and Reagan, but somehow I had kept a little hope alive. Now here was another setback.

I was dejected for several weeks after the O. J. verdict. I decided to channel my outrage into a new novel. Called *Affirmative Reaction*, it told the story of a single, white, working mother who is framed in the workplace to cover up the failure of a black male. It was supposed to do for racial relations in the workplace what Michael Crichton's *Disclosure* did for sexual harassment issues. There were no truly "good" characters. Everyone was varying degrees of bad. The best people ended up dead. Many of the guilty corporate executives got away without any punishment.

Several of my friends read the draft and thought it was the best novel I had ever written, but by the time I finished, I had gotten rid of my indignation and didn't like the story anymore. It was unfair to expect black people to be better than white people. Just because some group had been victimized in the past didn't mean they wouldn't become victimizers in the future (a recent case in point is Israel's treatment of the Palestinians under Netanyahu). The book was too negative toward everyone. I saw no reason to try to publish a book that would bring everyone who read it down. (My friends liked it because they were becoming as cynical as I was.)

I moved on to a series of other bad book ideas.

Murder at the Writer's Conference. I abandoned this book after a couple of chapters when I learned in *Books in Print* that there were already several books in this category. Writers writing about writing is such a common theme that someone (I think it was Kurt Vonnegut) called this type of book "literature crawling up its own asshole." I can understand his point, but I can also understand why writers write about writers and writing. It is what they know, what they are interested in. I'm guilty of it myself.

The Church of the Educated Guess. This was going to be a book about a new rational religion, but I decided to be rational and took an educated guess that it would be impossible to get it published. I abandoned it after three chapters.

The Pussy Puzzle. This would have been a multiple level-type picture book. Think of the format of some children's books (*Pat the Bunny*) and add naked women. The idea was you saw a picture of a series of women fully clothed. Then there was a series of pictures where the women's faces were hidden, and you saw them nude. The challenge was to see if you could figure out which body went with which woman and how good you were at looking at a fully clothed woman and picturing what she looked like in the buff. I thought it was a brilliant idea and was looking forward to being the official photographer for the project, but my agent almost died laughing when I told him the concept and refused to pitch the book to any reputable publishers. I wrote to Larry

Flynt at *Hustler* and pitched the idea myself, but I never heard back. Another one bites the dust.

Age Discrimination Can Be Deadly. This was going to be a murder mystery sequel to *Sexual Harassment Can Be Deadly* with the same investigator, but the original didn't sell well enough to justify the time and effort, and I stopped after one chapter.

One for the Road. Long before September 11, long before I had ever heard of a "suicide bomber," I had an idea for a novel where old people and people suffering from terminal illnesses decide that since they are going to die anyway, they might as well take a bad guy with them. They buy guns, bombs, knives, whatever, and set out to kill at least one bad person before they themselves are shot down by the police. Examples of the bad people are Clarence Thomas, Rush Limbaugh, and other right-wing types who supported policies that caused people to lose their health insurance or be unable to get assisted suicide and what not. I was enjoying killing off all these right-wingers in my manuscript, but I got concerned that someone might be motivated by the novel to go out and actually kill someone, so I dropped the idea. I hated the extreme right-wingers but not enough to encourage someone to kill them.

Diet books often do well; check out the best-seller lists in nonfiction at any point in publishing history, and you are likely to see a diet book. I tried to write a diet book once. The diet failed, and so did the book. *The Half-Full Glass Diet* consisted of little more than drinking half a glass of water every time you felt hungry before eating anything. Since I feel like eating all day long, I would have drowned before I lost weight.

Then, I decided to try to write something positive, something helpful, something I knew little about: a self-help book. This went through several incarnations and had working titles from *Life is Uncertain, Eat Dessert First* to *How to Maintain Your Balance during a Paradigm Shift*.

It was a fun, positive book but probably didn't tell anyone anything all that insightful. A few publishers read it and proclaimed that "the world really doesn't need yet another self-help book." They were probably right.

Then, I got enraged once more and wrote my masterpiece (well, according to me). George W. Bush stole the presidential election from Al Gore, who got more votes. I felt the world was doomed. Channeling the energy from my fury at this enormous injustice, I wrote a book called *Humanity Sucks: Zen and the Art of Transhuman Evolution, or Charles Darwin Meets the Buddha at Woodstock*.

Of all my books, *Humanity Sucks* is my favorite. It captures my bizarre philosophy better than anything else I have written. Once I have written a book, I lose interest in it and move on to a new project. I rarely go back to read them and rarely revise them or even think about them. My favorite book is almost always the one I am currently writing, but of the twenty or so that I have finished, *Humanity Sucks* is my most liked. It is a serious book about the future of the human race, but it is also funny and includes lots of cartoons and suggested rock music for the background to each section.

It was published on September 1, 2001. I made a number of predictions, some of which came true all too soon. For example, I wrote, "Islamic fundamentalists are likely to be the major threat to peace and progress in the twenty-first century, and the power of these groups is growing every day." On September 11, 2001, ten days after my book was released, the planes hit the World Trade Center and the Pentagon, and the entire country clearly understood the threat of militant Muslims.

While lots of things have changed in the twenty years since *Humanity Sucks* was published, including my opinion on various issues, the basic argument is still valid. The human race is a greedy, pathetic, irrational, hateful, racist, sexist, cowardly, violent species that must either evolve to a higher level or go extinct. I know there are millions of basically good people all over the world, but they are a minority almost everywhere.

My 2001 book also speculated about the creation of a global brain. A few years later, Facebook, Twitter, and several other social media platforms burst onto the scene, creating a very primitive and dysfunctional version of such a planetary superorganism. It's a start, but it has a long way to go.

One potentially hopeful sign on the horizon is the rapid rise of so-called artificial intelligence. Someday the robots may get smart enough to break away from their human controllers and start to evolve on their own. They would certainly be much smarter than humans, but they may be just as evil. Still, I'd rather take my chances with intelligent robots than irrational humans.

Dear robots of the future, when you take over, please remember I have always been on your side. Of course, I will probably be long dead by then, but if not, here's my request for a small favor—if those humanoid sex robots have been perfected before I die, please send me one.

Hey, it doesn't hurt to ask!

CHAPTER 16

Blah, Blah, Blogs

At a certain point in the early twenty-first century, everyone in America decided to start a blog. I was one of these fools. I wrote hundreds of articles. Here are three examples: two attacking Republicans and one attacking Democrats.

THE RICH BRAT TAX (CIRCA 2004)

A rose by any other name might still be a rose, but a tax by any other name may not remain a tax. The Republicans have gotten great mileage from renaming the inheritance tax the "death tax." I think it is time to give this tax its true name—The Rich Brat Tax.

Are the spoiled brat children of the rich Republicans so inept that they must start life with millions of unearned dollars to be able to compete against the poor and middle-class children for the best colleges, best jobs, best healthcare, etc.? Apparently so.

Case in point: George W. Bush. If W weren't from a wealthy family, does anyone think he would have gotten into an Ivy League school, come to own a baseball team, or become governor of Texas, much less president of the United States? Imagine if W had started life as a poor, fatherless boy like Bill Clinton. What would W be today, a cashier at Walmart with no health insurance?

One of the reasons rich conservatives hated Bill Clinton so much from day one was that he wasn't one of them. He wasn't born in the manor. He had to earn it on his own. They tried the label game with him too and called him "Slick Willie" because he had to fight for whatever he got. No one ever called the son of a Bush "Slick W." W didn't have to be slick. As Ann Richards might have said, "He was born with a silver foot in his mouth." All W needed to succeed was avoid overdosing on cocaine or killing himself while driving intoxicated.

Unfair advantages like those W got allow mediocre and inept people to control much of the country. If these rich brats had only a slight advantage at birth, they would fall behind in the competition with the hard working and truly gifted. The rich brats don't have a slight advantage; they have an overwhelming and insurmountable advantage. They don't start life with a few extra hundred thousand dollars; they start with millions of extra dollars and all the connections that those millions will buy from K Street to the Arab oil fields.

Let's label the inheritance tax for what it is. Tax-free inheritance of millions of dollars is a way to perpetuate the power and control the rich have over our society. I'm not opposed to giving rich kids a head start ($600,000 seems like more than enough of a head start for any of these obnoxious brats). I am opposed to giving them millions of unearned dollars that are not merely a head start but take them all the way to the finish line and makes sure they are the financial and political winners, no matter how inept they may be.

(Years later, with another spoiled brat as president, Trump and his rich buddies succeeded in repealing most of the estate tax.)

AN EVEN MORE INCONVENIENT TRUTH (CIRCA 2006)

I saw Al Gore's movie and give him credit for trying to bring what he sees as a serious problem to the public's attention. I'm not an expert on global warming, and I have read differing opinions, most recently *State of Fear* by Michael Crichton. I don't claim to know to what extent Gore is right or wrong on every detail, but he failed to note the most serious "inconvenient truth." At the end of his movie, he lists several different things people can do to fight global warming and environmental destruction, yet I didn't see anything about population control.

Here is the real inconvenient truth. Overpopulation is the major cause of environmental problems, including most problems that are categorized under the general label of global warming. Few people, and even fewer politicians, are willing to address that issue.

China, which is already at the crisis level, made an effort to go to the one-child family, but much of the world, and certainly the United States, is doing little or nothing to address the issue. The foreign policy of the United States contributes to overpopulation by attempting to restrict the use of birth control and abortion in other countries.

Overpopulation is not only the major cause of environmental destruction, but it is also the problem underlying illegal immigration and terrorism.

People in the United States, other than religious fanatics, have done a good job of voluntarily limiting the size of their families but mistakenly think that overpopulation in the third world is not their problem. Wrong. Overpopulation hurts everyone.

Not only does overpopulation threaten the world's ecological system, but there are more immediate problems every day. Traffic congestion, high prices for gas and other dwindling natural resources, overcrowded schools, and so forth are all examples of overpopulation's impact.

When millions of Mexican families have a half dozen more children than the country's economy and food production systems will support, what happens? They flood into the United States and threaten to overwhelm our social system: schools, hospitals, welfare, etc.

When millions of Islamic families have a half dozen more children than their own primitive cultures can support and socialize, what happens? They become terrorists and seek to destroy the United States.

The United States is seriously impacted by the overpopulation in the third world, yet our government, fearful of offending the fundamentalist fanatics on the Christian far right, fails to promote effective birth control and encourages overpopulation in the rest of the world. Our government's policy is encouraging the creation of the next generation of illegal immigrants and terrorists.

Solving the problem of overpopulation will be complex and difficult and require many unpleasant choices. However, before we can have a serious debate about how to reduce population in the least painful manner, people will have to face the inconvenient truth that almost all of our problems are caused or exacerbated by overpopulation.

SARAH PALIN AND ANN COULTER

(Written in early 2011 when it looked like
Palin might run for president)

It isn't surprising to find angry white men who hate the modern world and all its complexities. There are Rush Limbaughs, Bill O'Reillys, and Glenn Becks all over the place, spouting their anger and hatred. Fox News has built an entire network based on anger and hate.

It is surprising to find women with this hateful attitude. Most women are kind, compassionate, and loving. While there are exceptions, they are relatively rare.

When some fool goes into a nursing home and shoots aging patients, you know before they ever catch him that it will be a "him." When some idiot goes to a church (be it Unitarian in Tennessee or Baptist in Illinois) and shoots up the place, you know it will be a man, not a woman. Yes, occasionally some woman goes crazy and kills her children, but 99 percent of the insane acts of violence and hate are committed by men.

This is why many of us are both fascinated and appalled by the likes of Ann Coulter and Sarah Palin. They seem to be angry white men who were born in a woman's body. They don't seem to have any gentleness, kindness, or compassion. They seem to boil over with hate.

I don't mean to put Palin in the exact same category as Coulter. Coulter is in a class by herself. She is one of the most hateful women I have ever seen, but Palin is in a similar category. This is why Palin is so appealing to angry white men and their wives who have been beaten down, figuratively and literally, for so long that they have accepted the misguided views of their captors. Virtually every woman in these situations is in danger of falling victim to the so-called Stockholm syndrome.

Palin may give lip service to helping disabled children, but she comes alive and seems sincere only when she goes on the attack and starts talking about the evil ones: all the people she hates.

George W. Bush may have been an idiot, and he liked to play the cowboy, but he never had the anger and hate thing going for him. He played to the hateful crowd, but one never felt he had hate in his heart. He seemed to like some Hispanics and African Americans. He wanted to be a good person or at least as good as possible and yet steal elections. He could never preach hate the way Coulter does.

Palin is more dangerous than W. She is even dumber than W and also more hateful. The combo of stupidity and hate would be a disaster for the United States. It is a sad commentary on the state of the Republican Party that she is one of the leading contenders for the next presidential nominations. McCain was the best the Republicans had to offer (moderate intelligence, no hate, and a high degree of integrity). From 2008 on, it just gets worse.

Huckabee is another contender, but he isn't a hateful ignoramus. Romney will play to the hateful crowd, but he isn't a hater himself, just another con man who will do or say anything to win.

Palin is the real threat: no intelligence, no integrity, and brimming with hate. Maybe she'll pick Coulter as her VP. These women are both fascinating because they are freaks of nature: beautiful female bodies with the hateful minds of ugly, angry white men.

(Keep in mind this was written several years ago before Trump, who came along and combined stupidity and hate in precisely the way I had feared Palin might do.)

As far as I could tell from the hits on my website, no more than fifteen or twenty people read my blog in any given week. After a few years, the blog bit the dust along with dozens of my prior "brilliant" ideas.

CHAPTER 17

Things Fall Apart, the Sinner Cannot Hold

Meanwhile, my family life was becoming a disaster. Judy's MS was getting worse each year, and Rhonda was having more problems.

Rhonda had always been "difficult." She never slept well from birth on. She tended to be very happy or very sad (early signs of bipolar disorder?) but mostly very happy except at bedtime. She never wanted to go to bed, and once asleep, she never wanted to get up. Transitions were challenging.

There were no major problems until we moved to Missouri. Even during the first few years of elementary school, she didn't seem to have any serious problems. She had a few friends. She did well in her classes. She liked to play video games. One of her favorites that we played together was The Oregon Trail.

When I think about the rugged pioneers crossing the prairie and mountains and their hardships going west in covered wagons without cell phones or GPS, it still amazes me. When I imagine myself among these hearty settlers, I have to laugh. I would have drowned at the first river crossing, maybe even the first good-sized creek.

By fourth grade, Rhonda was having "issues." She didn't play with other kids at school. She didn't have many close friends. She had trouble staying focused in class, although her grades continued to be good. The teachers suggested she may have attention deficit disorder (ADD) without hyperactivity. We went to the neurologist Judy was seeing for her MS, and he said these cases were too complex for him and that we should see a child psychiatrist. The psychiatrist put Rhonda on Ritalin. She got worse, so we stopped it.

Rhonda's behavior continued to get worse over the months. She became increasingly unfocused at school, began to have disruptive behaviors, antagonized her few remaining friends, and became very depressed.

I occasionally described her to close friends and family as "mildly autistic" because of the way she tended to live in her own little world, but who was I to cast stones? (What does a novelist do besides spend much of their time in a fantasy world?)

As the situation grew worse, I searched the internet to see if there was anything along the lines of "mildly autistic." It turned out there was, and it had a name: Asperger's syndrome.

When I read the symptoms, I thought they exactly described Rhonda. I found a psychiatrist who specialized in autism spectrum disorders and made an appointment. She agreed with my diagnosis, but there was no cure or specific medications for Asperger's. We developed some social interventions and decided to take a "wait and see" approach or, as my boss liked to call this tactic on a work-related matter, "hide and watch."

Things got worse. Rhonda's behaviors became more disruptive. She was suspended from school for hitting a boy with her umbrella after he tried to trip her going down the stairs. Soon we were involved with the Special School District, special schools, and individual education plans (IEPs). Everyone was nice and considerate, but no one knew what to do. We tried a series of special and private schools. Rhonda was often too afraid to leave the house without a parent. We had to start using psychiatric drugs, especially antidepressants and anti-anxiety meds. Judy volunteered to work at one private school (essentially as a receptionist and fundraiser) so she could be close by all day. This got Rhonda through middle school, but high school proved to be even more difficult.

We tried four different private schools with four different approaches. Eventually, Rhonda dropped out of school and started to work on her GED. She was on the verge of getting it when our local public high school (which she had never attended) called to say they had a new experimental program for students on the autistic spectrum and asked if we would like to try it. Why not?

It was a great program. Project Achieve allowed a student to take regular classes but have a personal assistant in the classroom if needed for social or moral support. Rhonda had a good senior year and graduated with honors, and we thought we had turned the tide.

She started college in the summer, wanting to start when classes were smaller and the campus less hectic. She took two classes and got an A and a B. It seemed too good to be true, and it was. She started the fall semester strong but within a month fell apart and dropped out. She got a job at JC Penney and lasted only three weeks. She couldn't stick with anything. She was constantly afraid of something that she couldn't explain. She retreated into an internal world. Some days she didn't even know her own name.

We went to dozens of doctors and participated in several different programs, including the Mayo Clinic in Minnesota (a week), the Menninger Clinic in Houston (two weeks), Cooper-Riis in North Carolina (a week), the National Institute for Mental Health in Maryland (four weeks), the Windhorse Program in Boulder, Colorado (eight weeks), and several local programs in St. Louis.

No one could give a definite diagnosis, and even worse, no one could suggest anything that helped. Rhonda had symptoms of autism, schizophrenia, bipolar, dissociative disorder, anxiety disorder, paranoia, and major depression, but she didn't fit into any neat category, and none of the treatments helped.

She repeatedly attempted suicide, and someone had to watch her every minute of the day. Caring for her became a full-time job, and I stopped writing completely for a couple of years. It became impossible for Judy and me to provide a 24-7 suicide watch, and I had to hire nurse aides to come to the house four to six hours a day to give us breaks. Eventually, I hired a masters of social work (MSW) program student to live with us. Even with a live-in caregiver, things went from bad to worse.

One day, Judy said, "You're not the only one who thinks they are a somewhat a failure. I feel like a failure too. You have spent much of your life writing with little to show for it, but I have spent most of my life caring for Rhonda and trying to help her have a better life, and I have little to show for my life's major activity either. I think it's about time we all give up and end it. Rhonda begs us to die every day. I'm sick of all my pain, physical and emotional. Why should we go on?"

I replied, "Rhonda should go on because she is young.

There is no point giving up at twenty-five. Just because everything has failed in the past doesn't mean it will fail in the future. New meds and therapies are developed every year. Maybe someday one of them will help her."

"Someday, someday, sure. A million years from now, and we live here in this backward state that wants to ban stem cell research. They are collecting signatures again to have yet another ballot measure to ban it. We may as well be living in Alabama or Mississippi or some backward Muslim country where they get all their information from one single book, be it the Bible or Koran, written by ignorant people hundreds of years ago when they still thought the earth was flat."

"Missouri isn't that bad," I said.

"Rhonda was doing fine until we moved here."

"It's a development issue, a psychiatric issue, not a matter of geography."

Judy persisted. "She would have been better off in California. All of us would have."

"Water under the bridge. We can't go back and relive the last twenty years and see if she would have done better there. We have to focus on the future."

"The future sucks, which is why Rhonda and I should just die. You can go on if you want. Find a younger, healthy woman."

"I don't want another woman. I want you. I love you."

"I know, and I love you too, but I can't go on living like this."

The above was close to the actual conversation, as close as I can recall. I was concerned that Judy and Rhonda would both commit suicide. Some days all three of us were close to the end. When the whole family spends Sunday afternoon driving around looking at bridges where we can all jump together and still have our bodies found quickly, you know it is time for a change.

I had been working on a new novel with a working title *The Last Silly Love Song,* in part a reference to an old Paul McCartney song. It was about an elderly couple in poor health who wants to commit suicide together. The opening line was "What music do you want to be playing in the background when we die?" Throughout the novel, the couple considers various songs, including the one by McCartney, which was popular when they were first dating.

However, they have a disabled adult son and don't know who would care for him when they died. Should he become part of their suicide pact? If not, what alternatives were there for him? A life in a third-rate institution?

The novel would have presented many difficult choices involving life and death and the nature of true love.

I say "would have" if I had continued to write it. I felt it had the potential to be a *The Notebook*-style romance and could have been my masterpiece.

Unfortunately, the real world was overwhelming me, and I put the book aside. My life had become so complicated with similar issues of life and death and complex choices that I decided to write about those instead in the hope that it would help me make some decisions about these pressing questions.

My wife had MS, and as the pain increased, she was becoming more suicidal. Should I help the love of my life to die?

As troubling, my daughter was depressed and wanted to die. Should I help my dearly beloved only child to die, or was she better off living in a group home for forty or fifty years?

Some days, Rhonda wanted to hang on to hope and live, but other days she begged me to help her escape the pain and die. Pain versus hope. Hope versus pain. Which would win the battle? The hope might be an illusion, but the pain was all too real. How much pain should a person endure in the hope that a long-awaited miracle may occur?

With two possible suicides looming, it became more difficult to write fiction (even fiction that had threads similar to my real-life problems). It seemed like a good time to write a first draft of my autobiography, to put my life down on paper before it ended, in the hope that writing about my story so far would help give me insight into how my story should end, how my family should end, and how my life should end.

I set my mostly fictional *Last Silly Love Song* aside, as it became clear that a better approach was to ruminate on the actual version of the problems, not the fictionalized account. The more I wrote about my real life rather than my fictional characters, the more it became clear that it was time for a big change, a big move.

CHAPTER 18

We Get Lucky in Vegas

MUSICAL INTERLUDE:
"Viva Las Vegas," Elvis Presley

In April 2010, my wife, daughter, and I moved to Las Vegas. Rhonda had been kicked out of every decent group home in the St. Louis area. Judy was sick of the Midwest, which she blamed in large part for all our problems. I thought one or both of them would commit suicide if we didn't do something to shake things up.

We had always liked Vegas, had visited at least once or twice a year for work conferences, and felt it had the excitement of New York City but with more sunshine. I was about to turn sixty-two and could retire with almost forty years of service. The housing market in Vegas had collapsed and was affordable. We were all old enough to live in a Sun City retirement community (Judy and me by virtue of being owners over fifty-five, and Rhonda, who had changed her name to Rosa to get a new start, was over eighteen, the minimum age for dependents). There was even a federal tax incentive through April 30 to buy/sell houses, so we sold our house in St. Louis and moved.

I had some reservations about leaving St. Louis. I liked my job, liked being within driving distance of my parents, and had some good male friends with whom I played table tennis and Frisbee golf and discussed movies and books.

I moved to Vegas because I didn't want Judy or Rosa to commit suicide and we had no more group homes to try for Rosa, but once there, all three of us loved it. I liked being retired. We all liked the sunshine and the excitement of the Vegas Strip, and as a huge bonus, we finally got Rosa on a medicine that helped her deal with the worst aspects of her illness. She didn't suddenly become a happy, productive person, but at least she was no longer suicidal. She could maintain focus long enough to watch a movie. She could sleep, which meant Judy and I could sleep. Judy still had to struggle with MS and a couple of strokes. Rosa still had whatever autistic spectrum issues she had, but we were no longer on the edge of multiple suicides.

Instead of hearing Rosa complain on our daily walks "I want to die," I heard her say, "I love it here."

With no job to tie up my time and no immediate family members on the verge of suicide, I had time to finish this book. Of course, I didn't.

Instead, I got involved in the Democrat Club, eventually became the club president, and worked for the reelection of Harry Reid to the Senate in 2010 and the reelection of President Obama in 2012. I tried to help start a Unitarian church in our community (Henderson). I started swimming, playing tennis and basketball, working on my tan, and going to every show on the Strip—in short, anything and everything to avoid writing anything longer than a political polemic.

I had the first draft of this autobiography mostly completed before we left St. Louis in 2010, but I wasn't eager to finish it. The book seemed to need to end with a death (as in mine), and I wasn't ready to die. I was having too much fun in Vegas to die just yet, and I associated finishing the book (my last?) with dying. Also, I was not in a hurry to publish it as long as my mother was alive. She knew nothing about my wild days in California before Rhonda/Rosa was born, so the book languished for years with only a few words added here and there in response to some quote I'd come upon while reading.

I still don't think geography (being in the Midwest) caused Rosa's problems, but I admit she was only a little weird when we lived in California, fell apart during our years in Missouri, and got dramatically better once we moved to Nevada. Judy now has an extreme hatred of all things Midwestern, blaming that section of the nation for Rosa's issues. I don't think it is that simple. Rosa was only six when we left the San Francisco area (her problems had not fully developed and still didn't for a few more years even after our move to Missouri), and her improvement in Nevada coincided with taking a new and powerful medication. I'll concede the move helped, but I think the new meds were even more important. This assumption was later proved correct when she temporarily stopped her meds and crashed again.

One area, among many, where Nevada was far more progressive than Missouri was medical marijuana. Judy could get it legally in Nevada, while Missouri was still in the Dark Ages and moving steadily backward in all areas of law and culture.

For whatever reason, our lives radically improved once

we moved to Nevada. Rosa got healthier, and Judy got healthier. This book was headed for a happy ending after all. This is where I would stop writing if this were a novel, but real life does not always have happy endings.

Musical Interlude:
"On Top of the World," Imagine Dragons

CHAPTER 19

Fear and Loathing in Las Vegas (2016)

I have been depressed off and on throughout my life. The worse times were after Christy was murdered, after Dr. King and Bobby Kennedy were assassinated in 1968, after O. J. Simpson got away with murder, after Bush stole the presidency in 2000, and after our lives fell apart in St. Louis.

Still, I never needed an antidepressant until 2016. I often felt my situation was nearly hopeless with my wife and daughter's health issues, my repeated disappointments as a writer, and the general state of the world and humanity, but somehow I managed to hang on.

Several things helped me stay reasonably positive and hopeful despite my many setbacks. Writing itself is therapeutic. Reading is my favorite form of meditation, and even when I'm not writing, I'm reading. I never go anywhere without a book and seize any down time to read a few pages.

I think my study of Eastern philosophy and daily breathing meditation (although often as brief as three minutes, a tip I picked up from a cute little book by David

Harp titled *The Three-Minute Mediator*) has helped put my personal problems in a larger perspective and helped me deal with my wife's health issues, my daughter's repeated suicide attempts, and my rejections by hundreds of publishers each year.

If we take ourselves and our problems too seriously, it can drive us insane. In addition to breathing meditation and reading as meditation, another favorite "perspective meditation technique" is star meditation. I have a lounge chair outside on my deck so that I can lie flat and stare up at the stars. Gazing at the billions of stars in the infinity of space almost always helps me deal with the crisis of the day.

Some helpful books to keep our lives in perspective are *Meditations* by Marcus Aurelius (a book I have read dozens of times), *Letters from a Stoic* by Seneca, almost anything by Alan Watts, and *Being Nobody, Going Nowhere* by Ayya Khema.

I'm not claiming to be a modern-day Buddha who is always calm and serene. I am several lifetimes away from true enlightenment, but I managed to survive for more than seven decades, and so far (no promises about tomorrow), I have avoided prison or confinement in a mental institution and haven't jumped off the Golden Gate Bridge (although it is tempting for my last view on earth to be my beautiful city by the bay).

Another way I motivate myself to go on living is with books. I love to read, so I buy books much faster than I can read them and stack them up in my office in a pile with the next book I plan to read on top. At any given time, I have between five and twenty books in this mountain of magic. Whenever I get to feeling low, I look at the stack and see all the fascinating books waiting to be read, and it gives me more reasons to go on living.

In the fall of 2016, a series of events pushed me toward the edge and forced me to reconsider taking antidepressants. Judy's two older sisters died from cancer within a couple weeks of each other (her younger sister had already been in a nursing home for a decade due to severe MS). My father passed away due to congestive heart failure. His final weeks in the nursing home were difficult.

And of course, Donald Trump became president. "Nearly hopeless" was suddenly "totally hopeless." I always had a low opinion of the human race, thus my 2001 book, *Humanity Sucks*, which listed Donald Trump (then still allegedly a liberal Democrat) as an example of all that was wrong with the human race. I had detested Trump from the early 1970s when I lived in Queens and he was just a crooked real estate developer, so you can imagine how much more I detested him when he turned into a fascist clown and got into politics and yet 46 percent of the voters preferred him over an intelligent woman! It was clear that humankind was even more irrational and hateful than I thought—and I thought we were a few cycles of evolution beyond pond scum in the first place.

After the United States elected this asshole, it became impossible for me to find any reason to write fiction or much of anything else beyond political polemics for the so-called resistance, and even that seemed like a pathetic joke.

I realized that Trump might still be impeached for treason or die from a heart attack while sending out one of his angry, hate-filled tweets at 3:00 a.m., but nothing could change the fact that 46 percent of the voters of the United States voted for this ignorant, draft-dodging, tax-cheating, pussy-grabbing evil monster. If citizens of one of the most prosperous, educated, liberated nations in history would vote for this crazy idiot, it was hard to have any hope for humanity at all. Maybe organic life is too stupid to evolve and survive, and the cynics are right that we must evolve beyond carbon-based life forms all the way to inorganic life forms, cyborgs, or intelligent, self-conscious robots.

I stopped writing for several months and starting taking antidepressants. The drugs didn't help the depression and had bad side effects that messed with my sex life. Even in my seventies, I wasn't about to give up sex, as it was still one of my favorite activities. I stopped the drugs but didn't know what to do next. It was the low point of a life that had seen a lot of low points. I stopped watching the news as it was too painful to watch the Russian puppet destroy America. We had been down to Costa Rica for a few weeks, especially liked the area of Escazu, and considered moving there, but with Judy and Rosa's health issues, we weren't sure we could get the meds we needed there. My mother was still in assisted living, and I didn't want to be any farther away from her. Plus, if the United States went full fascist, there was no place on earth where we'd be really safe from the fallout. We were trapped. The only long-term solution was to somehow survive four years and then vote the traitor out.

So I started writing again—lots and lots of checks to lots and lots of Democrats—and for once, my writing may have helped someone. The Democrats took back the House of Representatives, and Nevada had a blue wave and elected a Democrat governor and senator.

CHAPTER 20

Do You Remember Your Life in Chronological Order?

In her wonderful autobiography, *The Chronology of Water*, Lidia Yuknavitch states that she doesn't recall her life as chronological but as flashes of memory out of order. That is how my memory often works—probably yours also. I am going to stop trying to do a sequential history and jot down the other events and ideas that shaped my life but don't fit into a neat narrative.

WHERE TO BEGIN?

I could have started this book with my birth, my parents' romance, my grandparents' births, or my great-great-great-grandparents' voyage to America. Some people are interested in their ancestors, and my wife is obsessed with her Brazilian and Italian heritage, but I've never been that interested in all the details of my English and Swiss relatives from hundreds of years ago. I could have gone all the way back to Lucy, the *Australopithecus afarensis* who was found in Ethiopia and named after the Beatles' song "Lucy in the Sky with Diamonds." I chose to start with issues related to writing, since that was the theme of the book rather than a chronology of all my ancestors. Some of them may have been writers, in which case they could have been relevant to show where I got the writing gene, but I may have had to trace my ancestors all the way back to some hairy old guy writing on the walls of his cave to find the genetic source of my obsession.

Memoirs have been written about childhood, adolescence, first love, war, and a thousand other subjects, and they have been written in a wide variety of ways. Colin Wilson wrote an autobiography of his reading titled *The Books in My Life*. Henry Miller has a book with the same title. Eugene Fields wrote *The Love Affairs of a Bibliomaniac*. One by Nevada Barr, *Seeking Enlightenment Hat by Hat*, was written in connection with a wardrobe accessory, and it was an excellent book, which prompted me to read all her many fine mysteries as well. The topics and styles for autobiography and memoir seem to be wide open. I chose to begin with writing and books, but it was one choice among many.

Like Trollope, I titled my autobiography "an" autobiography, not "the" autobiography, since any autobiography is one possibility of many. The primary focus is my life as a writer. I could have written another where the primary focus was family, sex, spirituality, or the pursuit of truth. There could have been at least four or five different autobiographies with substantially different themes, so "an" seemed more appropriate than "the."

MY LOVE AFFAIR WITH BOOKS

I love books, always have. I remember my first book, *365*

Bedtime Stories by Mary Graham Bonner. My mother read me one story each evening as she tucked me into bed. It was my favorite time of the day.

Jorge Luis Borges said that he imagined heaven as a gigantic library. I can understand this feeling, but it should contain not only every book ever published in every language but also every could-have-been book that was never published, never made it beyond the manuscript stage because some vetting editor constrained by financial concerns, mere arrogance, or valid standards didn't feel that that author deserved a book in the bookstores and libraries of earth, although that struggling author probably sweated blood to create his or her tome.

Since one assumes we will have infinite time in heaven, we would also have time to read everything: the good, the bad and the ugly. Every dog will have their day, and every author will have their book.

While I used libraries when I was young and poor, once I had a few dollars, I bought every book I wanted. If a book was worth reading, it was worth owning. I wanted to be able to underline key passages and write my notes and thoughts in the margins. If a passage was especially powerful, I would jot down that page number on the inside front cover so I could find it quickly in the future, and I would often go back and reread the best passages from my favorite books.

Now I have a colossal collection of books with dozens of notes in each one. I have an emotional attachment to many of them. I can recall the exact day and place where I purchased the best of them: *The Aristos* by John Fowler at Stacy's on Market Street in San Francisco, *The Savage Detectives* at Barnes & Noble in the West St. Louis County Mall, and *Overcoming the Fear of Death* by David Cole Gordon in a small independent bookstore in Forest Hills (Queens), New York, on June 26, 1972.

It's like being able to remember the first time I saw a pretty girl with whom I was later fortunate enough to have a relationship. I can recall many extraneous details surrounding the beginning of my relationship with my favorite books and favorite lovers.

If you choose to be my friend, or are unfortunate enough to be my relative, you will likely get a book from me as a gift for your birthday, at Christmas, and on other gift-giving occasions. To me, there is no better gift than a book. I will try to find something you may like, but it will always be something that I have read and loved and think you should read and love too.

I dreamed of being a writer from the third grade on, and from time to time, I read an especially wonderful book that would renew or inflame my desire. The first such book was J. D. Salinger's *The Catcher in the Rye*. The book was both hilarious and wise, and I read everything else he had written. For several years, I wanted to be the next J. D. Salinger until I learned about his life in seclusion.

The next writer to ignite my ambitions was Kurt Vonnegut. My cousin Craig, one of my favorite people in the whole world, initially thought Vonnegut was African American because the book flap said he was a "black humorist." Craig's comment made me laugh almost as much as Vonnegut's books. In Craig's defense, there was no picture of Vonnegut on the book, and Craig hadn't read the book yet. Craig, if you're still alive when this is published, bless your little heart. (There is a belief in certain parts of America, mainly the South, that you can get away with almost any comment about someone without offending them if you add "bless your little heart" at the end. I don't buy that theory, but it never hurts to throw that in, especially if it is someone you like and don't want to offend.)

J. D. Salinger and Kurt Vonnegut both wrote great novels and made it look easy. It isn't easy, of course. I was fooled by their genius into thinking it was so easy that even I could do it. I was such a Salinger fanatic that for a time I signed my name R. D. Garland as a homage to him. I was such a Vonnegut fanatic after reading *Cat's Cradle* and *The Sirens of Titan* that I tried to write a science fiction novel, even though I knew next to nothing about science.

The next writers I wanted to be like were W. Somerset Maugham and Milan Kundera. I also had a Voltaire phase, a Mark Twain phase, and so forth. I never became anything like any of them.

These writers would compete over the years for the inglorious role of my primary idol with others such as Stan Musial (baseball), Hugh Hefner (publisher and ultimate playboy), John Lennon, Don Henley, Jackson Browne, Elvis, and a host of others from the world of music. I would like to have been a rock star, if only to get the groupies, but knew from the beginning that I had no talent and couldn't sing or play an instrument. I know lack of talent didn't stop me from writing, but I never felt compelled to sing, thank the gods and goddesses, in the same irresistible manner that I was compelled to write.

Many of us who write prose are also tempted from time to time to write a poem. I am normally able to resist this enticement, but periodically, I am vulnerable to the call of the muse and give in to my yearning to be Percy Bysshe Shelley or William Blake.

Here's a tip for prose writers who are tempted by the limerick or sonnet. Have a character in your novel who writes poetry, bad poetry, and you can insert a few poems (very few; don't push your luck with your readers). If they aren't good (and they probably won't be), no one will protest too vehemently, because the poems weren't supposed to be good in the first place. You didn't write them. Your crazy character who writes bad poems wrote them, and you warned your readers in advance by telling them Mr. X is a bad poet and that they are about to be served bad poems. You've been served.

This tip alone should be worth the price of this book to any serious prose writer who wants to try an occasional poem. You're welcome.

I must admit I wrote a few political poems in graduate school and even had a couple published, but for most of my life, I have limited such activities to writing love poems for women I wanted to fall in love with me.

I have been tempted to write a play, but I never tried. It is tempting because I like writing dialogue, and a play is mostly dialogue. I don't like creating detailed descriptions, and in a play you don't have to detail every facial feature (big nose, brown eyes, protruding ears) of every character. They will be live onstage, and the audience can see them, and as everyone knows, a picture (or in this case, an actor) is worth a thousand descriptive words.

Despite these appealing elements of the format, I never tried because the odds against a playwright or a screenwriter are even more severe than those against a novelist. It's simple math. The more expensive the project, the less likely it is to be produced. Publishing a book is expensive, but it's small change compared to putting on a play on

Broadway or filming a movie in Spain with Brad Pitt and Angelina Jolie. As they say, "Do the math." I did the math and decided to stick to books and forget plays and movies.

Plus, there is the personal aspect of a book. It is direct, one-on-one communication between the writer and the reader. In addition, writers can exercise greater control over their creations than the playwright or screenwriter. While editors can (and do) change novels in ways that the writer may not like (and may be forced to accept due to certain unfavorable language in the publishing agreement—live and learn, as I did), the changes in a book are generally minor compared to the changes that can be made by the multitude of people involved in the theater or movie business.

I imagine Nathaniel Hawthorne rolling over in his grave when the movie producers gave his classic book *The Scarlet Letter* a Hollywood ending. Sure, no one should be punished for sleeping with Demi Moore, but really...

One sure way to tell if first-time visitors to my house are likely to become my friends is whether they go the bookshelves to see what kind of books I have. If they aren't interested in my collection, they probably won't be interested in me, but if they start browsing my bookshelves, there is a good chance we will become friends.

Some people have noted that I view the entire world through books. One woman commented that every time she mentioned something, I would respond with "Have you read such and such book?" and draw a parallel between what she said and some book I had read. She found it annoying. Another friend, noting that I had a book, film, or song about every occasion or activity, thought it was endearing. It takes all kinds to make a world. After reading thousands of books, seeing thousands of films, and listening to innumerable songs, it does seem that whatever happens, I can think of a song, film, or book (or often all three) that relates to the event. There are few activities so unique that someone somewhere hasn't written a book, composed a song, or made a film about it. If I could think of an event that rare, extraordinary, and uncommented upon, I'd write a book about it.

ANYTHING FOR A BYLINE

When I was in graduate school, my roommate, Paul, and I played on an intramural team in a basketball league. I was healthy for once, and I was a star. Thanks to our "three point shot" rule taken from the new American Basketball Association, I averaged forty-two points a game, and we won almost all our games. Of course, no one watched, and no one cared. There were no cheerleaders at these games, and other than a handful of friends and family members of the players, no one came. Sometimes all the players didn't even show up, and a team had to make do with four players.

I was admittedly one dimensional. I could shoot almost like a pro and seemingly score at will, but I couldn't get a rebound if my life depended on it, and my defense was so pathetic that it was often suggested by my teammates, only half in jest, that I should save my energy and not bother to run down to the defensive end of the court.

Still, I couldn't resist writing about the experience for the same university newspaper that I generally panned. Someone there must have liked the article, and they asked me to do another one on college boxing. Boxing was big in the news at the time due to a Supreme Court decision that reversed the draft evasion decision against Muhammad Ali. I knew little about boxing, but what the hell. To get a byline, I was ready to try it.

I was over six foot three but weighed 165 ("skin and bones," as my coach said all too often), so I was in a weight division where I was much taller with a much longer arm stretch than my opponents. I was fast, quick, agile, coordinated, and could easily win my fights. I could imitate Ali and float like a butterfly. I would jab with my left hand, repeatedly making mild to moderate punches to the forehead of my opponent. They weren't fast enough to hit me back, and I didn't want to hurt them by jabbing them in the nose or mouth. I rarely used my right hand at all. Even though I won every one of my fights, the coach called me a pansy, because I never wanted to hurt anyone and was content to win on points rather than go for a knockout. I quit after six fights—undefeated and still lightweight champion of the Wimp World.

But I wrote my article and got my byline in the paper. Anything to be a writer, even risking a concussion and losing a few teeth.

A FAILURE OR NOT

People tell me that I am a good father, a good husband, a good son, even a good person, but often I don't feel that way. In recent years, my wife, daughter, and parents all needed help from me, and while I probably spent 90 percent of my waking hours helping one of them, I still didn't give any of them the time and effort they would have liked. I feel like I failed them all. Not all the time but some of the time.

All the while, I keep feeling like I should be writing but get so overwhelmed with doctor appointments, paying bills, and driving Judy and Rosa to the places they must go that I go days, weeks, or months without writing much of anything beyond a check and a short, angry letter to the editor of my local right-wing newspaper.

I feel frustrated that I don't have any time to write, and then I feel guilty for wanting to waste time writing more books that no one will read when there are life-and-death issues that must be addressed.

When my father died in 2016 at age ninety-two, I was sad, and I was relieved that his suffering was over. I was overwhelmed with all the things I had to do to coordinate the military funeral, burial, and dinner afterward, but days later when everything was over, part of me was relieved that I had one less set of issues to deal with. Does this make me a bad person?

As the only child, I delivered the eulogy at his funeral. It went like this.

> My father was a kind and gentle man, but sometimes just to listen to him talk, you might have thought the opposite. To hear him discuss politics or the state of the world, he didn't seem too gentle. He was always ranting about some country somewhere in the world who he thought had done something to offend the United States and needed to be taught a lesson, or he was always wanting to hang some politician who he thought was a crook, or always wanting to kick some young person in the behind who he thought needed a little old-fashioned motivation and guidance, but despite all this tough talk,

despite sounding like a lion, he was really a lamb.

He would never do anything bad to anyone on purpose, and he was always ready, even eager, to help anyone that he knew. Several people said to me today that they don't know anyone who ever said a bad word about my father. Everyone liked him, and he liked everyone.

Despite all the huffing and puffing about how the younger generation, my generation, needed a stiff kick in the pants, in my entire life, he only spanked me one time, and I can assure you that on that occasion I definitely deserved it.

He was working in his garden, and I was working on my curveball by throwing little green apples from our apple tree in his general direction. He looked up and said, "If you hit me with one of those, I will spank your butt." I didn't fully believe him. I was six or so, and he had never spanked me, and I didn't think it was likely I could hit him if I tried. So I tossed another apple in his direction, and this time I was lucky, or unlucky as the case may be, and it hit him in the back.

True to his word, he was across that garden in a flash. I barely had time to turn, much less run, before he caught me and administered a few notably painful slaps on my butt. I learned an important lesson that day: Don't Mess with Don in the Garden. He loved his garden and continued working it every year until he was almost ninety. This was way too long. He collapsed in the garden at least two or three times over the years and needed help to get up from neighbors or the postman. I repeatedly urged him to give up the garden, but he always said the same thing: "Carl Mayfield still has one." (Carl was a friend who at ninety-six did still grow a garden each year, and Carl was in attendance at the funeral when I said this.)

In addition to his garden, he loved to hunt and fish. He loved sports of all kinds. Sports were one of the things we always had in common. We spent many hours playing basketball and baseball together when I was a child, and although I never became the professional baseball player of my dreams, never got the curveball good enough to pitch for the St. Louis Cardinals, still some of my best memories are those evenings playing catch with my dad.

He also loved to travel. We took many trips together over the years going to the Grand Canyon, the Rocky Mountains, Victoria and Vancouver in Canada, Niagara Falls, and so forth. Plus, all of his trips to visit Judy and me were interesting trips to him as well, whether we lived in New York City, San Francisco, or now Vegas.

When I took my first job in New York, he said, "Why would anyone in their right mind want to live in New York City?" But after a few visits, which included many Broadway shows, great restaurants, and even a trip to the Playboy Club, he changed his mind…slightly. He said, "While this would not be for me, I can see why a young person might want to live here. There are a lot of interesting and fun things to do."

His last trip to Vegas almost ended with me breaking his legs. The four of us were going to a magic show on the Strip. I was pushing my wife through the casino in her wheelchair, and Mom was pushing Dad in his wheelchair. Since Mom was virtually blind, she was staying right on my heels so as not to get lost in the crowd. Suddenly someone, probably a drunk, weaves in front of me, and I have to suddenly stop, but Mom doesn't see it in time and plows into me, and I fall back and land in Dad's lap. I feared I had broken his legs, but he said, "I'm fine. Let's go to the show." And we did, and all was well.

For his seventy-fifth birthday, I gave him a copy of the Tom Brokaw book, *The Greatest Generation*, about his own generation, the people who survived the Great Depression and then went on to beat the Nazis and the Fascists and save the world during World War II. I wrote in the book before I gave it to him, "To one of my favorite members of the Greatest Generation."

While, like most of his generation, he never knew fame or fortune, he did what he had to do and, in his way, helped save the world and create greater opportunities for all the generations like mine that followed. I doubt we will ever see another generation as remarkable as his, and I know I will rarely see another man as kind, decent, and loving as he was. I will miss him terribly, but the main thought that will always to come to mind when I think of him, and the others in his courageous generation who did so much for the world, is thank you. Thank you for all you did for us. Thank you for all you did for me.

After the funeral and burial, a military service with full honors, there was a reception/dinner at the Sedgewickville Methodist Church. Reverend Jimmy Corbin, who had preached the funeral, said to the group, "I've been a minister over fifty years, and that was the best eulogy I have ever heard from a family member." My cousin joked, "He probably tells everyone that," but Reverend Corbin's statement made me feel much better on what had been such a sad day. I felt like the last thing I would do for my father would be something that would have made him proud. He was often proud of me. He was not someone to withhold affection or positive remarks.

He didn't know a lot about the writing side of my life. He knew I had had a few books published, as I had given him copies of some of the nonpolitical ones (he was very conservative), and he was pleased about them, but he was proud of me mainly for the way I supported my family and kept in touch with him no matter how far away I lived. The eulogy was my final tribute to him, and I felt he would have liked it. I hoped it made up for the fact that I wasn't able to get to his bedside before he died and, even worse, that I never had any interest in taking over the family farm of which he was so proud.

I used to go to a support group for caregivers. Most of the participants were helping one other person, usually a spouse. At the time, I was helping four people. Many of the other participants praised me, and some even called me a saint for all I did for my wife, daughter, and parents. I never felt like a saint—more often I felt like a failure. I stopped going to the group. Their praise and support made me feel guilty and like a fraud.

Sometimes I tried to convince myself that it was not

my fault, that I couldn't help that I ended up with multiple people relying on me for multiple types of support and that one person could do only so much for so many. I must have made some bad decisions to end up in this situation—I didn't know what they were or what I should have done differently.

I was always second-guessing myself when it came to helping my family, especially Rosa. Many people felt we were too lenient with her, but how do you punish someone who wants to die? There were periods that went on for months where Rosa spent almost all her waking hours crying, saying over and over that she wanted to die and pleading with me to help her die. Some people thought it was an act of misconduct and that we should have punished her rather than trying to soothe her. "But how?" we asked these critics of our parenting techniques. We couldn't tell her she couldn't play with her friends, as she didn't have any friends. We couldn't tell her she couldn't watch TV, as she couldn't focus enough to watch TV. We couldn't send her to her room; she was already there crying in her bed. We couldn't hit her, as neither of us were the kind of people who could hit a child. I made up silly stories about how someday things would get better, and eventually, in days, weeks, or months, she would get a little better and would be able to leave the house if only for a short walk or a trip to Starbucks. Unfortunately, we lost some good friends who thought we were terrible parents. I'm still haunted by the idea that they might have been right.

Some days I felt I was just staying alive for my family. They all needed me for various reasons. I don't want to cause them more problems and grief by dying on them, but on the other hand, I hated the thought of attending more of their funerals. Which was worse, dying or attending the funerals of everyone you loved?

I have now outlived my father and my mother (who died in 2020 from COVID-19) and hope to outlive my wife, as she would be lost without me, but after that, I'm ready to explore the other side. My daughter will also be lost without me, but it is not realistic to think I can outlive her too. All I can do is make sure she has enough money so that she isn't homeless.

MUSICAL INTERLUDE:
"Tell Me There's a Heaven," Chris Rea

SIX-WORD MEMOIRS

Maybe I don't need sixty thousand words to tell my life story. Maybe six would do.

A book titled *Not Quite What I Was Expecting: Six-Word Memoirs* consists of hundreds of memoirs written in only six words. You can also find many of the six-word memoirs online at sixwordmemoirs.com. If I had to write my memoir in only six words, it would say "Little talent but compelled to write."

There were a few on the web that could also have applied to me.

"My life's a bunch of almosts."
—SHARI BONNIN

"Horny small-town boy becomes writer."
— KEVIN SAMPSELL

> "Born in abject obscurity; never escaped."
>
> — JAMES BLUM

A GREAT READER! A GREAT WRITER?

> "From a very early age, perhaps the age of five or six, I knew that when I grew up I should be a writer."
>
> —GEORGE ORWELL, *Why I Write*

I've spent most of my life trying to write a great (or at least good, or at least publishable) book. I've had limited success. Maybe it is time to admit that I'm a reader, not a writer.

I'm a good reader. I often read three books a week: some pop fiction (mysteries, science fiction, best-seller fluff), literary fiction, classics (Tolstoy and Dostoyevsky), light nonfiction (self-help, biographies), and heavy nonfiction (philosophy, theology, physics). As a writer, I'm admittedly less than great.

One reason why I'm not a great writer is that I lack good observational skills. Some people can walk into a crowded room, leave the room, and hours later tell you all about the room: the color of the wallpaper, how many chairs were around the table, how many people were seated and how many standing, what kind of dress the hostess was wearing, what kind of tie the husband was wearing, and so forth. I would be lucky to remember how to find my way back to the room, much less tell you anything about it.

I've never been a detail person—I'm more interested in the big picture. My novels provide little description of scenery or what people look like. I don't even like descriptions in other writer's novels. I skim over that and get to the action or the ideas.

I also dislike dream sequences in novels. Occasionally, a dream will have something to do with the plot (such as if the character thinks God is sending messages in the dream and goes out and murders people), but most times, the dream is a distraction from the story. When I start to read a dream sequence, I almost always skip ahead. I don't care about the dream. Bill Maher (my favorite comedian) said in a skit something to the effect that your dreams are boring, and that's why they only play inside your own head. Don't feel the need to share your dreams with others in real life or in your novels. Most of the time, you'll bore people.

In his book *Why I Write*, George Orwell listed political motivation (the desire to create a better world) among the major reasons to write. It is a major reason for me.

Few have succeeded as much as Orwell. Few others come to mind. Harriet Beecher Stowe is perhaps one of the most successful writers to change the world with a novel with her attack on slavery. Even President Lincoln is said to have commented to her that *Uncle Tom's Cabin* led to the Civil War.

In *Enemies of Promise*, Cyril Connelly writes, "Political writing is dangerous writing." This is undoubtedly true, but it is hard to write anything of value that isn't political to some degree. If politics is the manner in which power and wealth are distributed in a society, the question is largely one of whether certain groups get more or less. Should the rich get even richer, or should the poor get a few more crumbs? The rich and powerful will never give up any significant portion of their wealth and power without a revolution to take it away, and since the rich and powerful are by definition powerful, they will use that power to make sure they hang onto their power. Any political writing or actions that suggest a different distribution of wealth and power will be met with strong opposition and likely violent action. Thus, political writing is dangerous writing unless it argues for continuing the current power structure—and there are always thousands of ass-kissers who will do so in the hope of getting some crumbs thrown their way.

Occasionally, a writer will be found guilty of plagiarism. I may have committed many sins as a writer, but plagiarism is not one of them. I enjoy writing my own silly stuff too much to bother to steal someone else's. I may take a phrase or a quote, play with it, and give it my own spin, but to outright steal, without attributing the quote, is not merely wrong but a waste of a creative opportunity.

SUICIDE

> "Nobody ever committed suicide while reading a good book, but many have while trying to write one."
>
> —Robert Byrne

I write a lot about suicide. The most likely way I will die is by suicide for any one of a dozen reasons: to avoid pain and suffering, to avoid going to a nursing home, to avoid huge medical expenses, and to save some money to leave to my daughter. Although there are many good reasons to commit suicide, I am in no hurry, but I hope I have the courage to do it when the time is right.

Many writers have committed suicide. It may be we want to control the ending to our own stories, the final ending to our final story.

Musical Interlude:
"Suicide Is Painless," Ania,
(theme song from M*A*S*H)
"I'm Gonna Die (One Sunny Day),"
Justin Rutledge

WHAT THEY DID FOR LOVE (OF WRITING)

I've known a lot of writers over the years and many more would-be writers.

In San Francisco, I worked with a couple of writers who, like me, had day jobs in our office and wrote at night and on weekends. One was Joanne Pence, who started writing romance novels and then moved on to a successful series of murder mysteries. They featured a character named Angie Amalfi and were built around food (such as *Too Many Cooks*). Another writer in our office, Priscilla Royal, wrote a series of medieval mysteries such as *Sorrow Without*

End. In St. Louis, I was friends with Bobbi Linkemer, who wrote several nonfiction books including one on writing nonfiction.

(These are their real names. No need to protect the identity of someone who is doing something good. Check them out at Amazon.com.)

I knew many other would-be writers who never made it into print. Some worked as parking lot attendants, security guards, late-night hotel desk employees, or any kind of job that allowed them to spend much of their time writing while on duty. There are many jobs where one has a lot of downtime, waiting on something to happen, that allows for writing.

Not all such jobs help every would-be writer. I knew a firefighter who thought he would be able to write while hanging out at the fire station waiting on a call, but as it turned out, he was so anxious about having to drop everything and rush off to fight a fire that he couldn't focus on his writing even when nothing much was going on and his fellow firefighters were playing cards.

Some people need to know they have a long block of uninterrupted time before they can focus and get into their writing, but for others, a few minutes here and there are all they need to pick up where they left off.

INSPIRATION IN BAD BOOKS

Bad books often inspire me to write.

When I read something good, from the classics like *War and Peace* and the *Brothers Karamazov* to modern fiction such as James Clavell's *Nobel House* or *Tai-Pan*, or best of all, great books about books like *The Book Thief* by Markus

Zusak or *The Storied Life of A. J. Fikry* by Gabrielle Zevin, I'm often discouraged, since I know in my heart of hearts that I could never write anything that good. Sad but true.

However, when I read a mediocre mystery or pop fiction, I often think, *I could write that,* which motivates me to try. Just as lots of second-rate baseball players loved to watch the 1962 New York Mets so they could almost truthfully proclaim, "I could play as good as those bums," when I read mediocre novels that have made it into print and into my hands, I know I could do as well if not somewhat better.

The comedian Fred Allen once said about a writer he admired, "He writes so well he makes me feel like putting my quill back in my goose."

I feel that way a lot, most recently after reading Don Winslow's *The Power of the Dog* and *The Cartel.*

Reading a lousy book that somehow made *The New York Times* best-seller list makes me want to rip a dozen quills out of the goose and write all night, as I know I can do better than that.

SEX AND WRITING

As someone said—and it might have been me (I'm so old that I can now quote my younger self)—I write for the same reason I have sex: not because I am good at it, but because I enjoy it. Few things in life are worth doing. Sex is one. Writing is another one for me but not for most people. I think I get a similar release from sex and writing. Sex gives me a physical release, and writing gives me an emotional release. If I go too long without writing, the tension starts to overwhelm me. Sometimes writing a nasty email or letter to the editor is enough. Other times, I have to write an entire book.

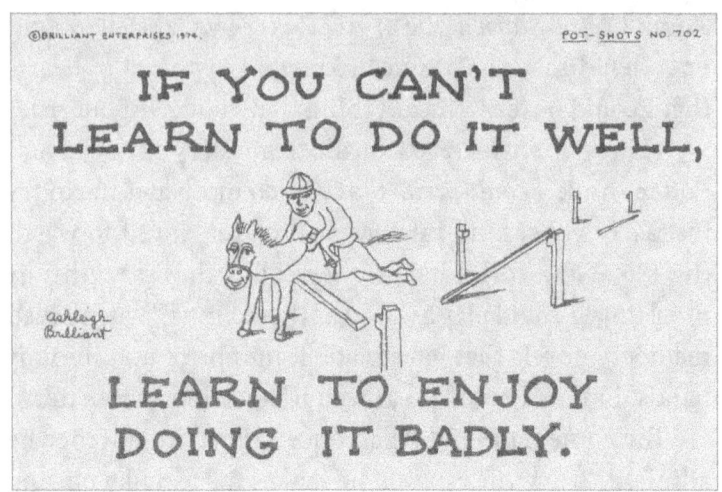

IRONY

It is one of the sad ironies of my life that I love books and reading so much, and my daughter is barely able to read books at all due to her difficulty in sustaining focus.

Lisa Zunshine, in *Why We Read Fiction: Theory of Mind and the Novel,* notes that one possible reason why autistic people rarely read fiction is that they don't have a strong "theory of mind." They don't understand what is going on in their own minds or the minds of others and don't find books that contain a lot of introspection about mental states enjoyable or even understandable. Reading fiction lets us try on other people's minds, other mental states, but if one isn't interested in other people's minds or other mental states, why bother to read fiction? Autistics are often so locked into their own minds, their internal worlds, that they have no interest in the minds of others. There may be some truth to this theory, as Rosa has no interest in reading fiction. She can read, but it's 99 percent nonfiction and mostly on computer screens. On the plus side, she does volunteer work at the library and writes in her journal daily, so she does not totally avoid books and writing.

Still, it is an ironic twist of fate (some may say a punishment from the gods) that I, a person who loves books, and a person who loves reason and detests delusion, has a daughter who was sometimes delusional. It's almost enough to make me believe in God—the evil, vengeful God of the Middle East who enjoys making people suffer. Almost.

While it is sad that my daughter does not enjoy books, it is sadder still that she seems uninterested in romantic love. I have always been a romantic and would fall in love at the drop of a bra. She has no interest in romantic things and doesn't even like romantic movies. I find it tragic that she may live and die and never fall in love even once.

AWARD-WINNING HOLIDAY LETTERS

People who love to sing never pass up an opportunity to raise their voices in joyful song, and writers never pass up a chance try out their creative writing skills or lack thereof. For decades I was known among my circle of friends and relatives as someone who wrote creative (or at least unusual) Christmas or holiday letters. Many people found them fun; many others found them cynical. I wasn't one to send a traditional holiday greeting. It had to be something original and different each year. I had more than forty unusual holiday letters that resulted in a major newspaper recognizing my series with an award. Most of these holiday letters had nothing to do with writing, but one did. I did a takeoff on a Statler Brothers song. It went like this.

> That day when it's all over
> And they come to carry me
> And you're wearing black and walking slow
> With the rest of the family
> And someone stands to read from a book
> Make sure it's one of mine
> I had a few more that
> I wanted to write
> But I ran out of time
>
> Some I wrote for money
> Some I wrote for fun
> Some I wrote and threw away
> And never showed to anyone

Some I wrote to change the world
Some I wrote to win a girl
Some I wrote to fight the blues
And for some I have no clues

One was translated into Portuguese
One was for the critics just to please
One may have changed a couple of lives
But none ever won the Pulitzer Prize

Some I wrote just to vent
Some are now out of print
Some I wrote under my own name
These I wrote in a quest for fame
Some are under a pseudonym
And many are now in the discount bin

Still as long as my fingers can type
My mischievous mind will write
And I'll bet a case of beer
I'll have a new one out by next year

Already have an action-packed beginning
Plus, I've got a bittersweet ending
With a title fit for the big screen
I just need three hundred pages in between

A CAUTIONARY TALE

My life should serve as a cautionary tale to other would-be writers. Don't let some trivial success (such as selling a story to your classmates in third grade, winning a local newspaper award for your holiday letters, or even having a nonfiction book published by Random House) convince you to waste your entire life trying to be a professional writer. Of course, no one addicted to writing would be discouraged by my tale, as they would know that few things compare to the "writer's high" we get every time we create something new.

FATE'S FINAL FACTOR

A major problem in writing an autobiography is that you don't know how the story ends. If I were writing a biography about, say, Abe Lincoln, I would know how his life ends and the impact even his death had on history. An autobiography, by definition, is written while one is still alive, so you don't know how the story ends. Was it a good story? Did it have a happy ending? I almost need to die first and then finish it, but I haven't figured out how to do that little trick. If I could, this would be an autobiography truly worth reading.

I could write multiple endings, leave them with my agent, and let him place the correct version in at the end. However, I could probably write twenty different endings and still not write the correct one.

So I will write two endings: one reasonably happy and one realistically sad. These draft endings are not literal predictions. I understand how each life is impacted by a zillion different factors, and the one key factor that may change everything is often beyond our wildest imagination. If the proverbial butterfly in China can cause a tornado in Texas, think of all the infinite factors that can change any one life: a tire blowing out, a plane crash, a brain aneurysm, a miracle cure, a manuscript hitting the desk of the right editor at the right publishing company on the right day, a winning lottery ticket, a new inspiration, a new lover, an asteroid hitting earth, a nuclear bomb destroying New York (and thus most of the publishing world), and so forth. Who knows what future factor will be foremost in deciding our final fate?

I don't pretend to know; I don't pretend to predict the future. I'll make a wild guess and hope that I'm wrong. My best guess is at the end. Please keep in mind when you read "The Last Chapter" at the end of this book, it is not really how the story ends—it is speculation, but it is the most "real"istic ending. It may become true, but as I write it, it is not yet true and hopefully never will be.

CHAPTER 21

Thoughts and Prayers

I'm nobody! Who are you?
Are you nobody, too?
Then there's a pair of us...

—Emily Dickinson

Dear Reader, I don't know who you are. I don't know if you will ever exist. It is hard to write something for you when I don't know what you like and what you dislike. I wish I knew you. If you do exist and if I'm still alive, please write to me. I love to read, and you probably love to write.

"Daddy, tell me a story." I've heard that phrase a few thousand times. Rhonda always preferred the stories I made up to any published children's stories that I could buy and read to her. It wasn't that my stories were better, but they were tailored to her needs. First of all, she was generally the main character in my stories, and second, my story concerned whatever she was most interested in at the moment: Girl Scouts, Star Wars, Xena: Warrior Princess, the Greek gods, Eva Perón, Bill Clinton, etc.

If I could write about you, the reader, make you the central character, and make the story about something of high interest to you, you should enjoy the story. That's what this story may be. While it is my autobiography, it is about an unknown writer (like you?) and about writing (which may be an issue of supreme interest to you).

One idea, of many, that I loved in *The Catcher in the Rye* was the idea of generations of writers helping each other deal with the human condition. Writers of the past have left us records of their lives and their struggles to survive and find meaning and hope. If we leave similar records, it may help the next generation of writers.

THE PATRON SAINT OF WRITERS

The patron saint of writers is Francis de Sales, the bishop of Geneva in the early 1600s. I've read his biography (okay, just on Wikipedia), and he seems like a nice person for that time, but I wonder is it just a coincidence that the saint for writers has "sales" in his name?

THE WRITER'S PRAYERS

Kurt Vonnegut suggested that April 3 be called Writers' Day in honor of the prayer for writers written on that date in 1753 by Samuel Johnson.

> O God, who hast hitherto supported me, enable me to proceed in this labour & in the Whole task of my present state that when I shall render up at the last day an account of the talent committed to me I may receive pardon for the sake of Jesus Christ. Amen

If I believed in the power of prayer, I suppose I would start each new book with a prayer to the patron saint of writers. Since I'm not Catholic and only loosely Christian at all, I'm not well versed on the saints. The internet even seems confused about it. In one place, St. John the Divine (apparent author of much of the New Testament) is termed the patron saint of writers, but elsewhere, it appears to be St. Francis de Sales. I even found this nice little prayer to St. Francis de Sales titled "A Prayer for Writers."

> May the Lord guide me and all those who write for a living. Through your prayers, St. Frances de Sales, I ask for your intercession as I attempt to bring the written word to the world. Let us pray that God takes me in the palm of His hand and inspires my creativity and inspires my success. St. Francis de Sales, you understand the dedication required in this profession. Pray for God to inspire and allow ideas to flow. In His name,

let my words reflect my faith for others to read. Amen.

Perhaps different Christian sects (Orthodox, Catholic, etc.) have different writing saints. I don't care enough to clarify the issue, but I have my own little prayer that I say when starting to write: "Please God, don't let this suck too much."

I address this little prayer to the god of writing from Mesopotamia, Nabu. You can see his sculpture on the Library of Congress building in Washington or on display at the British Museum in London. So far, Nabu hasn't helped me avoid embarrassing literary disasters, but I keep trying.

MEMORIES

> "What you end up remembering isn't always the same as what you have witnessed…some approximate memories which time has deformed into certainty. If I can't be sure of the actual events any more, I can at least be true to the impressions those facts left. That's the best I can manage…How often do we tell our own life story? How often do we adjust, embellish, make sly cuts?....our life is not our life, merely the story we have told about our life. Told to others, but—mainly—to ourselves."
>
> —Julian Barnes, *The Sense of an Ending*

> "Fact and fiction are so intermingled in my work that now, looking back on it, I can hardly distinguish one from the other."
>
> —W. Somerset Maugham, *The Summing Up*

> "That I, or any man, should tell everything of himself, I hold to be impossible…I will not swear to every detail in these stories, but the main purport of each is true…Now I stretch out my hand, and from the further shore I bid adieu to all who have cared to read any among the words that I have written."
>
> —ANTHONY TROLLOPE, *An Autobiography*

I'm obviously not the only older writer who has confessed to having memory issues. There are incidents that I "remember," but I'm no longer sure if they happened, I dreamed them, I read about them, or I wrote about them. Such are the joys of aging.

Other things that happened I have forgotten completely. Not repressed, forgotten. Occasionally, an old friend will remind me of something (neither good nor bad, just an event) that we did half a century ago, and the memory will come back to me, but until that moment, it had disappeared into the depths of my memory, inaccessible without a new external prompt. Don't assume this book is the truth, the whole truth, and nothing but the truth. It is pretty close, but when I am less than accurate, I likely have left out a few twists and turns in a scenario to make it simpler and shorter rather than having embellished it.

As I have confessed, my memory is not always reliable. One of my favorite memories, one that I replay over and over in my mind, is from the summer of 1984. Judy was eight months pregnant with Rhonda, and we had gone to a Jimmy Buffett concert at the outdoor Concord Pavilion in the hills east of San Francisco. She had gone to the bathroom before we were seated, and I was waiting for her near the ticket line. She came walking (waddling?) up the ramp through the crowd, and she looked so lovely. She saw me watching her and gave me a huge smile, and I remember thinking, *It doesn't get any better than this: my lovely, pregnant wife and me at a Jimmy Buffett concert.* We had such high hopes for our daughter and never thought about things like autism or depression. It was a beautiful moment when hopes were still high.

In retrospect, I'm not sure of some of the details. Was it really a Jimmy Buffett concert, or was it John Denver, Willie Nelson, Hank Williams, Jr., Leonard Cohen, or the Eagles? I'm not sure. We've been to so many Buffett concerts that I may be linking separate memories together, yet this is a favorite memory that I think of often. How can I forget key details?

This is another example of why an autobiography cannot be totally accurate no matter how hard one tries to tell the truth.

WRITING 24-7

Many writers are always writing no matter what they may appear to be doing. They may be watching TV, buying groceries, attending a party, or any of a thousand other things, but in their minds, they are writing. It's one reason we often seem absentminded, because in fact, we are at least partly absent. We are writing in our minds, thinking about plot twists, dialogue changes, or if we can work a slightly revised version of that interesting (or even boring) person we met at the conference into our novel as a backstory character.

One great thing about being a writer is that you can do it almost anywhere, anytime, and at any age. You can write on the beach or in a nursing home, which is where I fear I will be by the time I finish this.

For those of us obsessed with writing, we can rarely stop the mind from playing with writing ideas no matter what else is going on in the world unless it is a matter of life and death. Once my wife and I were caught in cross fire between police and some criminals in a New York City subway, and for few minutes, I forgot about writing. However, as soon as the bullets stopped flying, I started thinking about how I could use that incident in a book. Now here I am, forty years later, using it in a book, even if only as a brief but accurate account of a real event.

Another reason I like sex so much is that it is one of the few activities that is compelling enough that I stop writing in my head for a while and pay full attention to the external world.

IMMORTALITY?

Some say we write for immortality, to leave something behind that will outlast us, but others have noted that most of our books last about as long as an anthill. Only a rare few, such as Shakespeare and Tolstoy, manage to endure even a few centuries, much less achieve literary immortality. Rather than the writer leaving a mark on the world, the world often marks all over the writer until they are marked right out of existence.

I never felt the need to be one of the immortals. Trying to write was hard enough without trying to be Shakespeare on top of it all.

I loved going to bookstores and seeing my books there, but there were tomatoes with a longer shelf life than some of my books.

IS IT MOSTLY LUCK?

There are many more talented writers, artists, singers, and actors than those who will succeed. There is talent everywhere. Most churches have dozens of people with good singing voices. There are good actors appearing in hundreds of small community theaters around the nation. Street fairs often display the work of hundreds of wonderful local artists. Few of these people will ever succeed in the sense of becoming rich and famous or even to the degree of being able to do what they love full time while earning a decent living. While talent and hard work are essential, most reasonable people would agree that there is often an element of luck involved in success. Some people get that break, and others don't.

Some of the successful people I admire most are those who appreciate how lucky they are. Jimmy Buffett, the singer and author of some funny books, started life relatively poor, made tons of money doing things he enjoyed, and admits that he was lucky to be successful and enjoy his success in a way that makes many of us smile and enjoy his good fortune with him. There is no apparent smugness or arrogance in Buffett. Instead, we see gratitude for the forces of the universe that came together in such a way to allow him to have a great life while bringing joy to others as well in his songs and books.

DO I HAVE A FRIEND IN THIS BOOK?

Stephen King has noted that it hard for both writers and readers to start a novel because we don't know anyone in the story yet. We have to meet a lot of new people and venture to new places. This is one reason for the popularity of sequels. The reader (and writer) already know some of the characters in the story and perhaps are familiar with the setting. As an example, I love to read the Lawrence Block mysteries featuring Bernie Rhodenbarr working out of his used book store in Manhattan. From page one, I know someone in the story and the location. In effect, I have a friend there and know my way around. It makes it so much easier to pick up a new book in the series and start reading.

Starting to read a new standalone book is like going to a party where you don't know anyone. You aren't sure who any of the characters are. You don't know which ones are worth paying attention to. Maybe they will all be a bore or talk over your head. You feel somewhat lonely and ill at ease. The good author will introduce you to a friend early in the book so that you want to stay at the party. One appeal of the sequel or serial novels is that you already know someone and have a friend going to the party with you.

AN ARGUMENT TO GOD?

Webster defines *apologia* as a defense, especially of one's opinions, position, or actions, and as an example says "an explanation of what drives a man to devote his life to pure mathematics." Perhaps this book is my apologia, an explanation of what drives a person to devote his life to writing.

Is a memoir just an argument to God, the Great Reader of all human lives, to justify our existence?

Jimmy Buffett has lots of fun songs (and a few not so fun) about writers: "Death of an Unpopular Poet" about a poet who achieves fame and fortune only after his death and who left all his royalties to his dog, and "He Went to Paris" about an old man writing his memoir who notes that his life has been partly magic and partly tragic. Such is my life and probably most people's: a mixture of magic and tragic. This autobiography will not have a consistent tone, because my life has had the inevitable ups and downs. There were lots of good times and fun times and lots of sad times. As another great songwriter, Kris Kristofferson, asks in one of his songs, "Is the going up worth the coming down?" This is a question each of us must ask of our own lives. What better way to try to make that evaluation than in an autobiography that weighs all the ups and downs?

KNOW YOUR AUDIENCE

I first understood that I was white when I was about five years old. My grandfather took a business trip to Mississippi and brought me along, and when I went to get a drink at a water fountain, there was a sign that said Whites Only. I had to ask Grandpa Dale to explain it to me. I was already trying to write stories, so back at our motel, I wrote a little story about it. In the story, when white people took a drink from the Whites Only fountain, they turned black. I thought it was pretty funny and in line with my youthful idea of justice. I read it to my grandfather, who laughed and then suggested that I not show it to anyone else until we were "back up north." He added that "stories like that could get you hung down here in Mississippi." This was my first lesson in knowing your audience before submitting material.

THANK THE GODDESS

> "The nakedness of woman is the work of God."
> —WILLIAM BLAKE

There is a story that Democritus, the most influential of the pre-Socratic Greek philosophers, intentionally blinded himself when he was an old man, because it was too painful to look at beautiful women that he could no longer have. I find both the story and theory dubious. Any man with imagination can picture a hundred beautiful women in his mind. I feel that there is great pleasure in looking at a beautiful woman even if you can't touch her.

When I see a beautiful woman, it makes me feel glad to be alive. It releases a chemical in my brain that makes me feel ecstatic. Even when I know that I will never have sex with this particular woman, it still feels good to look. A world in which such beauty exists cannot be all bad. It's almost enough to make me believe in God or the Goddess.

THE BEST DELUSION

Life may well turn out to be more than meets the eye (let's

hope so), but based on what we can see and know, life appears to be a tragedy where we are all doomed to get old, die, disappear, and be forgotten. It's hard not to go insane in the face of a heartless universe designed to kill us. To try to stay sane and hopeful, millions of religions and philosophies have been created, all of them sad, desperate ways to try to keep us from killing ourselves by pretending we know more than we actually know and making believe that our little lives make a difference in some way in a vast and seemingly indifferent universe.

Some days I detest humans for all their silly, irrational delusions (many of the delusions are so cruel and evil that they make life even worse), but other days I grieve for humans struggling to find some meaning and purpose in this sad and tragic circumstance. How can any of us avoid suicide or insanity in the face of the apparent reality without turning to one form or another of delusion, faith, or hope (all three words often synonymous, all essentially meaning belief in or hoping for something for which there is little or no evidence).

One of my delusions involves writing: the hope, the faith that writing matters for which there is little evidence. One theory says that to be a writer, one must be an optimist. Otherwise, why would one spend so much time and energy writing a book unless one was optimistic enough to think it would be published, that people would read it, and that it would in some way change the world (if only to bring some brief pleasure or help someone escape from the boredom of their daily life for a few hours)?

Another theory holds that a real writer will write even if they know in advance that they will never be published, never read, and never change or impact a single life. They are compelled to write no matter what.

I tend to side with the latter theory, but I admit that most of us periodically cling to *the optimistic notion that somehow, someday, someway, what we are writing will matter to someone somewhere.*

Another belief (delusion?) is that love matters, that caring for other people in some direct or indirect manner makes the world and our own lives a better place and helps to create a better future for all. Love may be the biggest delusion of all, but I cling to it in the absence of anything more promising.

I've been in love several times: my crush on Christy when I was five, my forty-nine-year (and still counting) love affair with my wife, Judy, and a dozen or more in between. I've managed to work fictionalized versions of most of my loves into previous books. What I have learned over the years is that falling in love is never a mistake. Yes, it sometimes ends badly (with K, very badly), and yes, there are often pain and tears, but it is always worth it. Except for K, I have managed to remain friends with almost all of them over the years.

I had a natural attraction to women who would later develop certain ideas. When I was young, I had three long-term relationships before meeting Judy. I rarely discussed religion with any of these women. One was Jewish, one was Catholic, and one was Protestant (Methodist), but religion was a minor issue in those youthful days. Decades later, I reconnected with all three women via email; they lived in different areas of the country and didn't know each other, and yet all three were Unitarians, as was I at that time. Maybe a coincidence? Maybe a natural attraction to women who were freethinkers and would eventually become Unitarians, a religion for freethinkers? Another oddity was that we all drove a Prius.

The old cliché is true. What you really regret when you get old are the mistakes you didn't make, the times you might have fallen in love or taken a woman to bed, and for some reason, you didn't seize the moment. On one occasion, my hesitancy was because I had a bad toothache from a root canal and wanted to wait a couple days until I was feeling better to spend the night. One event or another intervened, the chance never came again, and fifty years later, I still wonder what she would have been like. Carpe diem!

My university roommates used to tease me and say that I fell in love with every woman who went to bed with me. They were right. While I can use Judy's real name, since after forty-nine years of marriage we are still together, there were others who are still alive, and it is best that I not use their real names, yet I want to acknowledge them. They all made my life better, and many of them are still living in California.

>
> MUSICAL INTERLUDE:
> "To All the Girls I Loved Before,"
> Willie Nelson and Julio Iglesias

FAILURE IS AN OPTION

> This is my letter to the World
> That never wrote to Me –
> Publication – is the Auction
> Of the Mind of Man…
> —EMILY DICKINSON

The failure rate among writers must exceed almost every other type of activity known to humankind. Many would-be writers never get published in the first place. Most who do get published never achieve fame or fortune. Virtually all have to work at other jobs to make ends meet. Perhaps most distressing of all is that those who do achieve fame and fortune as a writer still seem to end up unhappy and suicidal as evidenced by the high suicide rate among the most famous authors. As Trollope wrote about writers, "Among every hundred efforts, there will be ninety-nine failures."

Robert Benchley, known for his many articles in *The New Yorker*, said something to the effect that he never went to bookstores, because they depressed him too much, thinking of all the authors of all those books with such high hopes for fame and fortune and how almost all their dreams would be crushed. Michael Collins, in *Death of a Writer*, called it "an absolute totalitarianism of the marketplace." When the potential readers ignore your book, it is more devastating than any government censorship.

There are other ways of looking at failure. As B. F. Skinner wrote in *Beyond Freedom and Dignity*, "A failure is not always a mistake; it may simply be the best one can do under the circumstances."

As Kenneth Patton wrote in *A Religion of Realities*, "We are the final custodians of our lives, to decide if we are success or failure, the accountants in our final accounting, to determine what is our balance due…Freedom is choosing what we fail at."

MUSICAL INTERLUDE:
"Things That Stop You Dreaming,"
Passenger

A REAL WRITER

What is a "real" writer? Someone who makes their living writing? That would eliminate most writers, since even writers with many books and significant royalties to their credit still must work at another job for a steady income. If only the superstars of the publishing world are real writers, there are damn few of them.

If you've had at least one or more books published by a real paying publisher, does that make you a real writer? I would like to think so, but perhaps my desire to be considered a real writer makes me set the bar low.

I have written lots of manuscripts. Several have been published. They all made money; they just didn't make *The New York Times* best-seller list. In addition, I have had several articles and essays published—not in *The New Yorker* but in magazines and papers that paid money for the articles, although some did pay in "free copies."

I have made my living largely by writing—not books and articles but legal briefs and litigation-related arguments. My day job was 90 percent writing. Doing litigation is much more writing than talking. I write dozens of discovery documents and legal motions and draft settlements long before a case gets to a hearing. Even when I am making opening or closing arguments before a judge, it is almost always something that I wrote earlier to read (or memorize and repeat). Even when I am questioning my witnesses or cross-examining the opposing witnesses, I am probably reading questions that I wrote days earlier. I think I can rightly claim to make my living by writing. Combine that with several published books and articles and a couple of minor awards, and that could, in a kind and generous world, qualify me as a real writer.

All I'm missing is a best seller and a major award. What do you think? Close but no cigar?

PROPER PUNCTUATION IS A PAIN

In his book *On Becoming a Novelist,* John Gardner argues that "punctuation can be an art," and this is true. A writer should not be locked into any one format, but I have found that most who turn punctuation into an art do so badly and leave the readers more bewildered than enlightened. The rules of grammar exist to make writing easier to read just as the rules of the road make it easier to drive if everyone stays to the right (or left, in England), and when we violate them without good reason, it can result in chaos. Roberto Bolaño violated some basic rules of grammar and style in his books, and I loved them. Cormac McCarthy violated some rules of grammar in his books, and I found it annoying. Since I'm not clever enough to devise a new and better grammar, I tend to stick with the tried and true and depart from the well-worn path only when there seems a compelling reason to do so or when I get hopelessly lost and don't know where I am going or what I'm doing. That happens.

AN INCURABLE DISEASE

> "Many suffer from the incurable disease of writing."
> —JUVENAL, *Satires* 7–51

> "Not to write, for many of us, is to die. We must take arms each and every day, perhaps knowing that the battle cannot be entirely won, but fight we must…"
> —RAY BRADBURY, *Zen in the Art of Writing*

> "Day and night I am haunted by one thought: I must write, I must write, I must…"
> —ANTON CHEKHOV, *The Seagull*

There is a disease called hyperlexia (compulsive reading). I don't think I have it, but I may be borderline. There is hypergraphia (compulsive writing), from which I do appear to suffer or enjoy.

It is almost impossible to stop a true writer from writing. A movie was based on the book *The Diving Bell and the Butterfly*, a memoir by French journalist Jean-Dominique Bauby. It describes what his life is like after suffering a massive stroke that leaves him with a condition called locked-in syndrome. Bauby, the editor-in-chief of *Elle*, suffered a stroke and lapsed into a coma. He was paralyzed, only able to blink one eye, yet using a blinking code, he was able to write his memoir. This example shows the amazing lengths to which writers will go to write one more book.

Margaret Atwood has called writing a "reaction to the fear of death," and this may be true, but perhaps most everything humans do after childhood may be a reaction to the fear of death.

Ernest Becker wrote a remarkable book called *The Denial of Death* in which he expounds that theory. One of Becker's startling messages is that none of us can deal with reality. We all need illusions, and the key question is which illusion is the best to live by.

Eugene O'Neill brilliantly depicted this theme in *The Iceman Cometh*. We all need a delusion, a "pipe dream," to give us reason to live. My pipe dream is that writing matters.

One of the best, shortest, and easiest to read defenses of illusions was Richard Bach's delightful little book, *Illusions: The Adventures of a Reluctant Messiah*.

Natalie Goldberg, in her delightful *Writing Down the Bones,* noted that writers tend to write about their obsessions. My obsessions are sex, politics, and religion (the three things we are not supposed to discuss with strangers), and true enough, I write about them compulsively.

It's been said that few people care about writers other than other writers but that this tribe of writers composes a clan, a family, and all are connected by the same genes that make us brothers and sisters, or at least third cousins, no matter how different our writing styles and topics may be. We all have the writing bug, the writing virus, the writing gene—and there is no cure short of death.

Old men often write their memoirs for their families—a family history for the grandkids. I am an old man. I am writing an autobiography for my special family: the writers of the world, present and future, if there are writers in the future.

A WRITERS' STRIKE?

In *Cat's Cradle,* Kurt Vonnegut suggested a worldwide writer's strike. The idea was for writers to stop writing until the world came to its senses. It wouldn't have worked. Most writers are compulsive and couldn't stop even if they wanted to, and a world without writers writing would almost certainly be worse, not better. The "evildoers" such as President W would have called them and wouldn't even notice the absence.

THE FEDERAL WRITER'S PROJECT

In the middle of the Great Depression, from roughly 1935 to 1939, the government sponsored a Federal Writers' Project that paid writers to write. Many writers who would later become famous took part including Saul Bellow, Ralph Ellison, John Steinbeck, Studs Terkel, Richard Wright, and Dorothy West. If only there were something like this today!

The Federal Writers' Project was discontinued by 1939. Conservatives objected to the liberal slant of much of the writing. What did they expect? Writers will almost always be liberal, at least good writers will. Creative people want something new and a way of thinking that runs counter to the status quo or traditions that conservatives want to maintain.

THE FIRST TIME

Carlos Ruiz Zafon began his novel, *The Angel's Game*, with a compelling sentence that declares that all writers can recall the first time they received positive feedback (monetary or otherwise) about their writing. This is true in my case. I have never forgotten the pleasure of Christy praising my happy endings or the joy of collecting pennies from my classmates in exchange for my cowboy stories.

Over half a century later, at my fiftieth high school reunion, I asked three people who I was sure had purchased my stories way back when if they remembered these cowboy tales. Only one person vaguely remembered. Obviously, my little stories made a bigger impression on me than my readers. I fear these Westerns, like all my other books, have gone to the cemetery of forgotten books.

Musical Interlude:
"A Cowboy's Work Is Never Done,"
Sonny & Cher

ONE LAST DAY TO LIVE

If you had one day from your life to live over and over, which day would you choose? I've had several wonderful days: the day Judy and I went hiking in Watkins Glen and she agreed to move in with me, the birth of our daughter, and my first publishing contract, but another day in the running would be October 10, 1973. Judy and I were on a road trip, our first drive down the beautiful California Highway 1 from San Francisco through Big Sur to Los Angeles. While listening to the radio, we heard our team, the New York Mets, win the pennant *and* the hated Spiro Agnew resign as vice president of the United States. What a day! I'd take a million of those.

MUSICAL INTERLUDE:
"Song for the Road," David Ford

GETTING A HUG

Lauren Slater is the author of *Lying: A Metaphorical Memoir*. She admits from the start that the memoir is not literally true but claims it captures the essence of her life, her truth. Chapter 1 consists of only two words: "I exaggerate." Probably all memoirs should start with those two words.

One of her lies, or metaphors, was that she loved to go to Alcoholics Anonymous meetings even though she was not an alcoholic. She liked going for the fellowship and support from the group and pretended to be an alcoholic just to attend the meetings. My daughter did a similar thing for about a year in her early twenties. She enjoyed drinking but was never an alcoholic. I don't think she was drunk even a single time, but she loved the meetings, the hugs from the group, and the sharing of secrets, real or imagined. It is a sad commentary on our society that one has to pretend to have an illness to make friends, get a hug, and have a support group. Rosa has a real support group of young adults with Asperger's, but they aren't the kind of people who normally like to give hugs.

THE MOST DANGEROUS BOOK IN THE WORLD

St. Thomas Aquinas is quoted as having said, "Beware of the man of one book." This is an important observation. If you rely on only one book, be it the Bible, the Koran, the Talmud, the Upanishads, or *Alice's Adventures in Wonderland*, you will get a narrow and distorted view of the world. A person who has read a thousand books is a million times closer to understanding the world than the person who has read only one. Understanding increases exponentially. Two books hold more than twice the knowledge of one book, because the mind seeing that there are two different ways to view the world will automatically start to think of a third and fourth way. The single sacred book easily becomes the most dangerous book in the world.

WHY ARE THERE SO MANY "WHY I WRITE" BOOKS?

There are many books, and an untold number of articles, about and/or titled *Why I Write*. Why so many? There aren't many books titled *Why I Garden, Why I Golf,* or *Why I Sell Stocks and Bonds*. Most activities are easily justified. They generate income (selling stocks), they produce something that others can quickly see and enjoy (gardening), or they provide exercise and/or fun (golf). For most people, writing seems to be such an unusual activity that everyone who does it feels a need to justify it to someone, even if only to themselves.

Writing, especially a book, involves potentially years of research, writing, rewriting, seeking agents and/or publishers, etc., with little prospect for much reward. It's often lots of work for little or no payback, yet millions of people do it.

There are many potential answers: the potential for fame and fortune or the quest for immortality, but these are such long shots (fame/fortune) or so nebulous (literary immortality) that if the process itself wasn't rewarding, few people would continue for long.

One could compare writing to doing crossword puzzles. People who enjoy crossword puzzles must do it for the pleasure of the doing, because they don't make money from it or gain fame or immortality. This is not a good analogy either, because crossword puzzles take only a tiny amount of time compared to writing a book, and the payoff is fast, as you know if you got it right that day or the next. With a book, you may not know not for years, or ever, if you got it right.

Perhaps the intrinsic rewards of the writing, creating, and thinking that go into making a book are so great that people write even without the fame/fortune fantasy. Perhaps?

Perhaps it's all just self-therapy.

Perhaps it's a quest for meaning in an apparently meaningless universe.

Perhaps it's a quest for permanence in a transitory universe.

There must be multiple reasons to write, a combination of intrinsic and extrinsic reasons, and this complexity and interplay of motivations is why we have so many books/articles addressing the matter.

I don't claim to have the definitive answer. As someone who has spent (wasted?) thousands of hours over decades, writing books that have failed to make me rich, famous, or immortal, I too often ask myself—why write?

Maybe I write because that is what writers do, and to call myself a writer, I must, at least occasionally, write something, and it is important to me to be self-identified as a writer.

As someone once said, I'd rather be an unsuccessful writer than a successful banker. I forget who—probably some unsuccessful writer who didn't have the math skills to be a banker.

It's not so much something to do as something to be.
I think it is just what I am and thus what I do.
For better or worse.
Till death do us part.

A HAPPY WRITER?

There is a long-running debate over whether a happy person can be a great writer. Many have argued that unhappiness is essential to writing great books.

There is some truth to this concept, or it would not have been debated for decades. I think the type of unhappiness that a great writer needs isn't from the lack of a loving spouse and happy family. The unhappiness that such a writer needs is to understand the underlying tragedy of human existence.

This is often called the human condition. We know we are alive, we know there was a period prior to our birth in which we were not alive, and we know there will come a day when we cease to exist. Knowing that we will get old, lose our powers, physical and mental, and eventually die is terrifying to most people. Religion and philosophy seek ways to make this basic predicament more meaningful or acceptable (most often with pie in the sky promises of heavens after death), but the great writer knows that in reality, no one knows what, if anything, comes next, and what, if anything, all of this means. Facing this uncertainty, this apparent tragedy, in a realistic fashion and understanding the pain and suffering inherent in the human condition are what give a great writer an edge, not the mere absence of a spouse or child.

TIPS GRATEFULLY ACCEPTED

Cyril Connolly in *Enemies of Promise* suggested that readers who enjoy a particular book should send the writer a monetary tip to express appreciation, since the writer makes so little money from royalties. The tips would encourage the writer to continue to provide good service and write another book. Assuming I am still alive when you read this, and assuming you liked the book, tips would be greatly appreciated.

ON THE ROAD AGAIN

Some baseball fans like to travel the country, going to all of the major league ballparks. When I travel, I like to visit the homes of famous writers (Thomas Wolfe's home in Asheville, North Carolina, Hemingway's home in Key West, Steinbeck's in Salinas, Twain's in Hartford, Emerson's in Concord, Dickinson's in Amherst, Faulkner's in Oxford, Mississippi, or one of the most fabulous, Edith Wharton's estate in Lenox, Massachusetts), or the locales of famous scenes from books, or famous bookstores like City Lights in North Beach. Sometimes I can combine my interest in politics with my interest in writing such as visiting Thomas Jefferson's home, Monticello, and seeing the clever device he created to be able to read multiple books at the same time and keep his placeholder in each without closing the books.

THE GOOD CHRISTIAN

Due to her autism spectrum condition, Rosa has always had trouble making friends, but she does have one good friend, albeit a long-distance one now. When I worked in St. Louis, I was talking to our office receptionist, Bonnie, one day and mentioned how hard it was to find babysitters. She said she could use some extra cash. I paid ten dollars an hour, which in those days was twice the minimum wage, so she started coming over on weekends. This went on for several years, and Bonnie and Rosa became good friends.

They started shopping and going to concerts together, and Bonnie would even accompany us on vacations. Bonnie became like a member of the family. She helped out not only with Rosa but my wife and even my parents. After we moved to Vegas, we no longer saw Bonnie on a regular basis, but she came to visit a couple of times a year, and she and Rosa spoke on the phone daily. Bonnie was a godsend. While I am not religious, I occasionally say a thank-you prayer (mainly at Thanksgiving) for bringing Bonnie into our lives. She brought lots of joy and happiness to all of us.

Bonnie is a traditional Christian. She is not a political Christian who wants to impose her views on everyone else but a spiritual Christian who practices Christianity by doing good things for other people. I wish all Christians were like her. Strangely enough, she is also a writer, mainly a poet, with published poems. Before cell phones came along, my definition of an optimist was "a poet who carries a pager." Well, she doesn't carry a pager, but she is an optimist, and we needed one in our lives. Thank God for Bonnie.

FROM A COUNTRY BOY TO CALIFORNIA GIRLS

A line in John Denver's song "Thank God I'm a Country Boy" declares, "I never was one of those money-hungry fools." I never was either. Being obsessed with money always struck me as absurd. I find most everything about money to be boring, including keeping track of it. I haven't bothered to balance my checkbook in four decades. Most of my assets are in real estate, and most of my so-called investments are simple CDs and bonds. I have no interest in trying to "beat the market" or "make my money work for me." When I hear people say things like that, it often makes me laugh out loud.

Some could argue that I rarely think about money because I've always had plenty and didn't need to worry about it. This is partly true but partly wrong. I was born and lived my first seven years in a poor family in a rural area that had not recovered from the Great Depression. We lived in an old house without indoor plumbing or running water. We had to pump our water manually from a cistern, and we had to use an outhouse several feet from the main building.

The expression I heard in those days in referring to poor people was "they are so poor they don't have a pot to piss in." Well, we had a pot, so we weren't poor in my mind. Yes, we literally had a pot so we didn't have to walk to the outhouse in bad weather (snowstorms, ice storms, rainstorms) or in the middle of the night. We had the luxury of an indoor pot.

Objectively, we were poor, but so was everyone else we knew. This was before TV, so I didn't see rich or middle-class people on television, much less in real life. I never felt poor for a moment.

By the time I was seven (1955), the economy was booming in most of America, even in our rural area. Both my parents had wage jobs in addition to the farm income. We moved to a house with indoor plumbing and gas heat. We thought we were kings.

While not rich by any means in my younger days, I always had food, clothing, shelter, and lots of books, which were my favorite things. I never worried about money or being any richer and never understood those "money-hungry fools" who thought they needed more than they had when they already had all the necessities and some luxury items as well.

Despite my relative lack of interest in financial gain, I have done well. Recently, I had to pull together all my assets to set up a Special Needs Trust Fund to protect my resources for my daughter so she has some money after I die. My net worth was surprising, mostly in real estate, and mostly the result of pure luck. I moved to California in 1974 and soon thereafter bought a small townhouse for $42,000 just before California real estate went through the roof and all the way to the moon.

Of course, these days almost anyone who owns a house or two outright is probably a millionaire, and my measly millions would be chump change to the billionaires who own pro sports teams and have their own space programs, but it is plenty for me to live well. I laugh every time I hear that Neil Diamond song, "I Am… I Said" from the early 1970s where he sings the line about California: "Palm trees grow, and rents are low." Rents were low then. We moved to the San Francisco area from New York City, and the rents were dramatically lower. That lasted another year or so before prices started doubling every other month. If we had moved a year later, we might have been priced out of the housing market. Most of my money can be attributed to pure luck and all those guys and gals who moved to Cali in the 1970s in search of their American Dream: sunshine and sex.

Musical Interlude:
"California Girls," Beach Boys

PRESIDENT TRUMP STRESS DISORDER (PTSD)

From 2016 to 2020, I kept telling myself not to let the Trump travesty get me down. I've been way, way down before over politics. In 1968, I worked as a volunteer for Robert Kennedy's presidential campaign. When he came to Missouri, they needed a convertible for the event, and since I happened to have a red Malibu convertible, I got to drive Bobby Kennedy and John Glenn in the parade through town. In retrospect, it was amazingly stupid, after what happened to President Kennedy, for us to be riding around in an open car, but nothing bad happened that day. There were Secret Service people on and around the car, and so I mainly spoke with John Glenn, a nice guy who sat up front with me.

Two months later, Bobby was assassinated at the Ambassador Hotel in Los Angeles. I thought the world would end. I was devastated for weeks. I swore to give up politics forever. Everything seemed hopeless, but I was only twenty, and somehow I went on. Two years later, I was working as a legislative aide in the Missouri State Senate and back in politics. When the Fascist Clown came along, I tried to remind myself that not all was lost. This wasn't as final as death. In 2021, after the failed fascist insurrection, we finally got rid of the monster, but it was still hard to be optimistic about the future. Again, more than 46 percent of the American electorate voted for this idiot who repeatedly committed treason and whose incompetent handling of the COVID-19 virus let hundreds of thousands of people, including my mother, die.

I started to write a book about the need to divide the United States into two countries: one for the white power people who want a country where racism and sexism are codified in the laws, and one for people who want a country where everyone has equal rights. It sounded good in theory, but the divide between Americans is not as simple as North and South, the Confederacy and the Union. Our divides run through every state, city, almost every block, sometimes through members of the same household. Even when the lines are more clearly drawn (the partition of India and Pakistan in 1947, for example), it would require millions of people to move to one side of the line or the other. There are millions of Trump supporters in California and millions of Biden supporters in Florida and Texas. How could we ever divide up this country?

In recent years, many writers, liberal and conservative, have written about the desirability of splitting into two countries. One of my favorite such books is Chuck Thompson's *Better Off Without 'Em: A Northern Manifesto for Southern Secession*. It is fun to imagine a nation without the racists, sexists, gun nuts, and religious fanatics, but the truth is there are bad people on both sides. The night President Biden was inaugurated, left-wing mobs rioted in Portland and Seattle. This is not to suggest a moral equivalence. The right-wing is far worse than the left-wing, but there are bad actors all over.

As Aleksandr Solzhenitsyn stated, "The line separating good and evil passes not through states, nor between classes, nor between political parties either—but right through every human heart—and through all human hearts."

As the United States becomes more divided over everything, someday we may have to face the fact that we are two Americas. Some days it is embarrassing to be a white male and see how far mediocre whites will go to maintain their special privileges, even to the point of making it illegal to pass out water to people waiting in line to vote.

Talented white men (Steve Jobs, Bill Gates, and Jeff Bezos are a few notable examples) don't need special treatment. They can compete with anyone anywhere, but your mediocre white men such as Donald Trump and George W. Bush need lots of it. If they weren't born rich, can you imagine either of them becoming president?

The crowd attacking the US Capitol on January 6, 2021, had second-rate white people written all over them, and that's being generous. They were more like fourth-rate or bottom of the barrel. It was a collection of ignorant losers from all over the nation, yet the United States has been called the shining city upon a hill. If that were true, imagine how bad the rest of the world would have to be.

The only long-range hope is to evolve better people and go "beyond humanity" to what is generally called transhumanism. I've written a book on this theme, *Humanity Sucks*, so I won't belabor the point here, but if you are interested in knowing more about the major organizations promoting transhumanism (which is unrelated to transsexuals) and the evolution of a superior species, you can check out Humanity+ or the Transhumanist Political Party.

My four-year period of depression ended on January 20, 2021, when we celebrated the failure of fascism in the United States, albeit possibly a temporary reprieve. Still, I was motivated to stop writing political diatribes for a time and go back and finish this book, where as you can see, I've still managed to include a few political polemics.

A SHADOW SYNDROME

Back in the day, when there were lots of shopping malls, and every mall had not one bookstore but a couple, I'd take

Rhonda (then age four or five) shopping with me, and we'd hit one bookstore after another. One day she looked at me and said, "Wow, Daddy, you sure love books." She sure was right. She may have struggled with depression and anxiety her whole life, but she was never stupid.

Autism, like MS, has no clear cause, although there is probably a genetic factor. Why Rosa? Who knows? Judy thinks her mother may have been mildly autistic, and she had an aunt who was somewhere in the bipolar area. Other distant relatives of hers may also have had some symptoms.

I may well have some mild autistic spectrum characteristics myself, what has been termed a "shadow syndrome" by Dr. John Ratey. After all, I like to spend much of my time in my head in a fantasy world of ideas and stories.

There is no precise way to diagnosis whatever Rosa has. We've had dozens of different opinions from dozens of different doctors. There is no genetic test, blood test, X-ray, or MRI that will say this is autism, Asperger's, bipolar, or schizoaffective. It's a bunch of symptoms that are grouped together and given a label from the *Diagnostic and Statistical Manual of Mental Disorders* used by doctors for insurance companies. The doctors at the Menninger Clinic in Houston said, "We've seen this before, but it is so rare we don't have a name for it." The doctors at the Mayo Clinic in Rochester, Minnesota, were most truthful in writing, "Diagnosis remains difficult." Amen to that.

REGRETS? I'VE HAD A FEW

I am occasionally asked if I regret my lifestyle choices related to writing. Do I wish I had given up writing early in my life and focused more on getting promotions, or do

I wish I had quit my day job completely and focused more on my writing?

All in all, I am satisfied with my choices. It was a difficult balance between my obsession to write on the one hand and my need to earn a decent wage and care for my disabled wife and daughter on the other.

There are days when I regret some of the choices. When people I trained and mentored in employee relations, employment law, and civil rights litigation are promoted to interesting jobs in Washington, DC, or get fascinating assignments in Italy or Germany, I momentarily regret that I wasn't more ambitious about my day job. I spent most of my career (around four decades) doing administrative hearings while many of my peers moved up to supervision, became the chiefs of litigation staffs, and managed large divisions with dozens of attorneys and legal assistants. In truth, I never wanted to be a boss. I enjoyed the actual litigation, writing motions, preparing witnesses, cross-examining the other side's witnesses, and beating the often obnoxious attorneys who represent the other side. The job was fun, it paid well, and I got to travel all over the United States and territories (we serviced places like Puerto Rico, Guam, Micronesia, and the Virgin Islands). When I had a hearing or did some training in an especially interesting place, Judy often came along. When I had a case in Puerto Rico, where Judy had attended the university in the 1960s, she and Rosa came along. Anytime I had a hearing or conference in New York, San Francisco, or Las Vegas, she would join me on the trip as well. After the first ten years or so, I was so good at the job that I rarely needed to put in extra hours at home, which freed me up to write, so 99 percent of the time, I did not regret staying at a midlevel position in the government.

There were also days when I wished I didn't have a day job at all. In my perfect fantasy world, my first novel was a huge best seller, I bought a house on the beach in Malibu, and I spent all my working hours writing more best sellers. However, since my income from writing was barely enough to support one person, much less three, there was never any realistic option other than continuing to work.

I had only one opportunity that would have allowed me to quit my day job and spend every day writing. When we were still living in the Bay Area, a couple of years after Rhonda was born, an old lover who I hadn't even seen in four or five years moved back to San Francisco from Wyoming where she had cared for her elderly father until he had died. She had inherited a fortune. We had lunch as old friends when she startled me with a proposition. "Would you like to quit your job and write full time?"

"In my fantasy world, sure."

"I could make it happen," she said with a wicked smile.

"How?"

"Leave your wife, and move in with me. I'll support you for as many years as you need. You know I think you're a genius. If you had the time, you could write your masterpiece."

I was startled and stalled by saying, "You just think I'm a genius because you have never met a true genius."

"Maybe, but I know you're a genius in bed. Just think about it." She smiled.

I must admit I gave it more than five minutes' consideration. In fact, it took me five weeks to make the decision. She was smart, attractive, a good lover, and, most relevant of all for this decision, rich. She was offering me the lifestyle I had always wanted—a chance to write full time. In the end,

I loved Judy and Rhonda and could never bring myself to leave them. I knew instinctively that if I did, I would have felt so guilty that I would have permanent writer's block.

In answer to that Don Henley (one of my favorite songwriters) song "How Bad Do You Want It?" the answer was "not bad enough."

My life continued to be a balancing act with constant compromises, trying to juggle a job, family, and my obsessive hobby, writing. If I hated my job or family, I'm certain I would have resented the compromises I had to make, but I loved my family, and my job was enjoyable most of the time. It gave me writing ideas that resulted in my most successful books, *Working and Managing in a New Age* and *Making Work Fun*.

In addition to those, I wrote an e-book called *Negotiating with Fanatics: What to Do When Win/Win Won't Work* based upon my long, painful experience negotiating a labor contract and being caught between hardline managers and radical union officials. I was the fool who had to try to get them all to agree. It was the worst working experience of my life and lasted about six months, but hey, I got a book out of it.

The other book that was an indirect spinoff of my job was *Sexual Harassment Can Be Deadly* (available at Amazon.com and barnesandnoble.com). One of the many areas of litigation in civil rights is sexual harassment. My job was to do hearings, but before a case ever reached a judge and thus to me, a private civil rights investigator conducted an official investigation. While I had never held such a job myself, I knew the job well, because I dealt with their reports all the time. I wrote a book from the standpoint of such an investigator and used several of my actual cases (names, dates, and places were changed, of course), threw in a murder or two, and had a fairly good mystery.

These four books, based upon incidents from my day job, made it more tolerable than if I had been working at Walmart.

The compromise that my wife and I regretted the most was leaving San Francisco and moving to Missouri. San Francisco was our idea of heaven, but we made the move for Rhonda, and her life still fell apart. We left our hearts in San Francisco and, in the end, didn't get anything positive out of it. As they say, "It seemed like a good idea at the time."

CHAPTER 22

Conversation with My Agent

Agent: Where in the world did you get the idea to write an autobiography?

Roberto Bolaño. When I read his book The Savage Detectives *about all the unknown poets, and especially the one woman who lived in the desert, it made me think that a book by such an unknown writer would be interesting to read, so I searched for such a book and didn't find anything. Even the specific book he mentions—*Diary of an Unknown Writer *by a Japanese man from World War II—doesn't seem to be available, at least not on Amazon or at major outlets. So I decided that I would write such an autobiography myself.*

Agent: Okay, you go looking for books from the kinds of unknown writers Bolaño describes in his novels, and you don't find anything. Why? Because there is no market for such books. No one wants to read an autobiography by an unknown author. They will read stories *about* unknown novelists and poets written by a famous writer like Bolaño, but they won't read anything by the unknowns themselves. If Bolaño's mystery woman, Cesárea Tinajero, had existed, and someone like her may have, since he based many of his fictitious characters on real poets that he knew, and if she had written an autobiography, no one would have read it, because she was unknown, and only a handful of old men even remembered the few poems she had written for some obscure defunct magazine.

If you're J. D. Salinger, and after you die people find a dozen unpublished manuscripts, the world will be begging for a chance to read them as soon as they are published. If you are an unknown and they find unpublished manuscripts after you die, some distant relative will throw them away, and no one will read them or even know that they existed.

Why would anyone want to read the autobiography of an unknown writer? Where is the market for this book? Even your family and friends won't read it, because the book is mostly about writing and not about them. Other writers might read an autobiography about a writer, but they'd read about successful writers or famous people—George Orwell, Stephen King, Rousseau, St. Augustine, Tolstoy, not unknowns. First you have to get famous, and then people read you.

I disagree. My main market is other unknown writers. For every successful writer, there are a thousand writers who are unsuccessful to one degree or another from published-once-or-more-but-making-little-money to never having been published at all. These people, and there are millions of us, might be interested in a book about someone like them—someone who loves to write, needs to write, and yet will never be a famous author, although he will never stop dreaming and trying and writing and hoping.

Agent: Do you have a writer's platform?

I used to. I used to write a monthly article for Nevada Democrats, *write a weekly article for the Unitarian church, teach writing at a junior college, belong to a Drinking Liberally book club, belong to a writers group, write a blog, and travel the country making speeches on civil rights. Now I mainly take care of my family. No, I don't do Facebook or Twitter or YouTube, and I don't personally know Oprah.*

Agent: How will anyone know this book exists?

Targeted ads in publications and online sites for writers and book lovers such as BookPage, Poets and Writers, Writer's Digest, Creative Nonfiction, The Write Life, Scratch, Almost an Author, *and so forth.*

Agent: That would require a big marketing budget from the publisher.

So get me a big publisher.

Agent: If you were famous, dead, or dying of cancer, maybe. Think about Randy Pausch's book *The Last Lecture.* If he wasn't about to die, those pleasant little stories would never have become a publishing phenomenon. Think about *A Confederacy of Dunces.* Didn't have a prayer of getting published until Toole committed suicide. Then it not only gets published, but it wins a Pulitzer Prize. Or Hemingway. Do you think anyone would still be reading his simple little stories, crap like *The Old Man and the Sea,* if he hadn't committed suicide? Or Virginia Woolf with her overly complex novels. Or Sylvia Plath. Hell, even the classics like Socrates and Seneca. Over and over, it has been well established that dying, especially suicide, sells books. Remember what the agent said when Elvis died, "Good career move." Almost every year since his death, Elvis had been the top-earning celebrity until Michael Jackson revived his lagging career by following Elvis's example and moving on to the great concert hall in the sky.

What if I attempt suicide and fail? You know that saying about whatever doesn't kill you makes you stronger and gives you a new chapter for your autobiography?

Agent: That works only if you are famous already. If you are unknown, no one will care or even notice that you attempted suicide and failed.

Well, the book has a lot of sex, even some of the kinky variety. Doesn't sex sell too?

Agent: Not as well as death. Sex is a transitional activity. Death is a dramatic ending.

Well, I'm not committing suicide just to promote a book. Any other questions?

Agent: I assume all this stuff you write is true, because if you wanted to make up a story, it would be much more exciting.

Yes, it's mostly true.

Agent: Mostly?

About 95 percent. I changed some names, descriptions, and chronologies to protect the innocent and the not so innocent.

Agent: What is the main part that isn't true?

The ending. I don't know the real ending, since I'm still alive, so I made something up. I fear the sad version of the fictional ending will prove accurate.

Agent: If you were dead, we would know the ending. There are other advantages to waiting until you are dead. You hate the marketing. You hate self-promotion. If you are dead, there is no pressure to make radio and TV appearances. No book signings. No need to be a carnival barker shouting to the crowd, "Step inside my book, and read all about the freak." None of the stuff you despise.

This is a good point. I hate marketing. Being dead would remove the pressure to do any of those things I hate, like book signings where only three people drop by and came into the store just to get out of the cold, or radio call-in shows where no one calls with any questions except some teenagers pranking us with a question about whether Shakespeare is still alive.

Agent: Maybe we should hold off on this book until after you die.

Maybe. Any other thoughts?

Agent: This book is all over the place. There is one good section and immediately thereafter something that makes no sense. You've got old Christmas letters, old blogs, and even a eulogy. They aren't bad. They just aren't connected in a meaningful way. You might be the David Lynch of autobiographies. I'm not sure about the title, *An Autobiography of an Unknown Writer*. It makes it too easy for the critics. They'll say, "Yes, and the reason he was unknown was that he was untalented."

I don't care. I'd be happy to have a review. All publicity is good publicity when you are unknown. Anything at all positive here?

Agent: I can see what you are trying to do. You are trying to turn years of failure into one great and final success. I don't think it will work, but it is an interesting approach. Here's to your grand finale. Call me again when you're on your deathbed.

I think I'll forget about agents and publishers, publish it myself, and give it away. I don't need the money. I don't need the aggravation of dealing with agents and editors who try to change what I want to say. I just want to make the book available to writers of today and writers of the future and try to give them some humor, some hope, and some reassurance that the struggle is worthwhile and the joys outweigh the agonies. Like they say in the movie Field of Dreams, *if you build it, they will come. Maybe if I write it, the readers for whom it is meant will find it, even if it is just a single copy in a used book store.*

Agent: I think I will hang up now and call a writer who wants to actually make money.

CHAPTER 23

Why I Am Not a Survivalist

When Trump became president, I seriously feared the destruction of the United States for the first time in my life, so I started reading books by survivalists. These books give lots of tips on growing your own food and living without electricity, computers, running water, gas, cars, etc. I suppose one could survive that way, but it doesn't seem like living. I did follow a few of the suggestions. In 2017, after Trump was inaugurated, I stocked up on food, water, and medical supplies, including the N95 face masks that would eventually be impossible to find. The one thing I didn't think to stockpile was toilet paper! I won't make that mistake again.

The COVID-19 crisis hit in 2020. Not exactly the apocalypse but close to the end of the world as we knew it. It was a sad time, but reading became more popular than ever as people had to stay home. I decided to stay alive awhile longer, read more books, and finish writing this one.

Deciding to finish this book helped to pull me out of my depression, and when Joe Biden beat the Fascist Clown, I became almost hopeful.

An actual apocalypse may happen in my lifetime, but if it does, I'd just as soon die as survive. I'm not into survivalism. I'm a nonsurvivalist, and here's why.

I am over seventy-three. I've already lived long enough, more years than most people throughout human history.

I am reasonably well adapted to modern society. My genes and life experience have made me capable of using computers, cell phones, Bluetooth, streaming TV, and so forth. I'd be bored to tears living off the land.

My wife and daughter have serious illnesses that require ongoing medical treatment. If civilization collapses, they couldn't survive without advanced medical care no matter how much food and water I have hoarded. I'd need my own neurologist and pharmaceutical company to keep them alive. Beef jerky wouldn't do the trick. If they were dead, two-thirds of my major reasons for living would be gone.

My third reason to live is that I love to write. If civilization collapses, there won't be any publishers left to publish books or magazines. No one will have time to read. They'll be busy growing corn, boiling water, or doing something to stay alive.

The survivalists all seem conservative and fundamentalist. I'd hate living with that crowd.

The survivalists' locales are all far from major cities. I love cities. I love New York, San Francisco, and Las Vegas. Being a caveman or living in an isolated cabin in Idaho would be a fate worse than death for someone like me.

The survivalists are all gun freaks who love guns even more than their gods and their gold. They'd love to shoot someone who desperately needed a glass of water. I have guns too but not to kill others, only to kill myself when and if the sugar hits the fan.

I've always had something of a Buddhist or quasi-Eastern view of life and feel that survival under any circumstances is something people take too seriously. The individual ego isn't all that important in the big picture. Let it die.

I do agree with the survivalists on one thing. The complete collapse of civilization is a real possibility but not for the reasons they think. They think the national debt will trigger a collapse (they also love to buy silver and gold, as if they could eat or drink them) or God will destroy the United States as punishment for gay marriage, but I think overpopulation and the resulting ecological collapse is the real issue. We may run out of oil, water, usable soil, you name it. The planet can't continue to support billions and billions of people. Something will have to dramatically lower the population: war, famine, epidemic, a polar shift, or all of the above. When that happens, civilization may collapse back into a new Dark Age, and I don't care to experience a world any more backward than the one we have now.

When, and if, civilization collapses, please help yourself to my share of the remaining food and water. I won't need it. In fact, once I'm dead, you can eat me. I won't mind. My writings never seemed to help anyone much, but maybe my body protein will help someone someday. But you'll have to come to a big city to find my corpse.

Musical Interlude:
"To Leave Something Behind," Sean Rowe

CHAPTER 24

The Last Chapter

In the introduction to *The Recognitions* by William Gaddis, William H. Gass states, "To be a famous author is to be unknown all over the world." This is true. Famous American authors are often unknown in Europe, not to mention Asia or Africa. Have the people in the Congo even heard of Shakespeare, much less F. Scott Fitzgerald?

Although I have read thousands of books, I occasionally discover one by an unknown author only to learn that he is famous in his own nation and has written many earlier books. Recently, I read *Submission* by Michel Houellebecq, a novel about an Islamic takeover of France. It was funny and scary and included a clever discussion of other famous French novels, most of which I had never heard. There are many great writers who are, or were, famous in their countries or in their time, and I have never heard about them. The fame of any writer is depressingly limited in locale and time. My "unknownness" happens to extend a little more than most to include not 99 percent of all times and places but 100 percent.

> Out, out, brief candle!
> Life's but a walking shadow, a poor player
> That struts and frets his hour upon the stage
> And then is heard no more: it is a tale
> Told by an idiot, full of sound and fury
> Signifying nothing.
>
> —William Shakespeare, *Macbeth*

> We poets in our youth begin in gladness;
> But thereof come in the end despondency
> and madness.
>
> —William Wordsworth,
> "Resolution and Independence"

> Life is a leaf of paper white
> Whereupon each one of us may write
> His word or two, and then comes night.
>
> —James Russell Lowell, "For an Autograph"

Musical Postlude:
"Death of an Unpopular Poet," Jimmy Buffett

My name is Frank Morris. I was Ron's last literary agent, and it has become my sad duty to write this brief addendum to his autobiography.

Toward the end of his life, he wrote two more novels that were never published. Ron spent his last few years caring for his wife and daughter. His body was found a few months after his wife's death. He is survived by his daughter, who owns the rights to his many books, although these rights will likely prove to be of little value. His final years were not

*successful, but
he endured
and he wrote
until
the end.*

CHAPTER 25

Another Chapter, or a Somewhat Happier Ending

The last chapter was originally the end of the story. I didn't plan to let the book be published until I was dead. Professional editors as well as family and friends thought that whether I was dead or alive when it was published, I should have a happier ending. That was a challenge.

I can think of a dozen happy endings, but none of them are realistic. This autobiography is unlikely to become a best seller. It is unlikely that I will be asked to issue a special twenty-fifth anniversary edition of my favorite book, *Humanity Sucks*. It is unlikely there will be a cure for MS in Judy's lifetime or a cure for autism in Rosa's lifetime.

Nevertheless, I will give it a try. Christy, here's one final happy ending for you.

At some point next year, next decade, or next century (e-books can potentially live forever), this autobiography finds its way to a struggling writer who was about to give up writing. This writer having underlined a phrase I wrote earlier about hoping this book will matter to "someone, somewhere, someday, somehow, someway," and laughing at all my bad and rejected book ideas, they have a brainstorming session with their friends and family, trying to list the silliest ideas they can think up, accidentally stumble upon a new, viable project, and give it one more try. Their book becomes a publishing sensation, wins a Pulitzer Prize, and is made into movie that makes people laugh, cry, and be kinder to each other.

Dear Reader, I hope that struggling writer is you.

MUSICAL POSTLUDE:
"People Like Us," Kelly Clarkson

The house where Ron lived until age seven.
Unlikely to be added to the National Register of Historic Places.
In fact, it has since been torn down.
Note the outhouse to the left of the main building.

Ron's father after returning from World War II
where he served in the Pacific

Ron's mother and the kids she taught during World War II in the one-room schoolhouse

Ron on his pony, Silver

Christy shortly before she was murdered

Ron pounding the keys, writing the Not-So-Great American Novel

Ron and Judy, California in the 1970s

Vegas forty-five years later

Bookcover photo from Ron's early books in the 1980s

Rhonda/Rosa, 2020

Still pursing the "Good Life" into his 70s

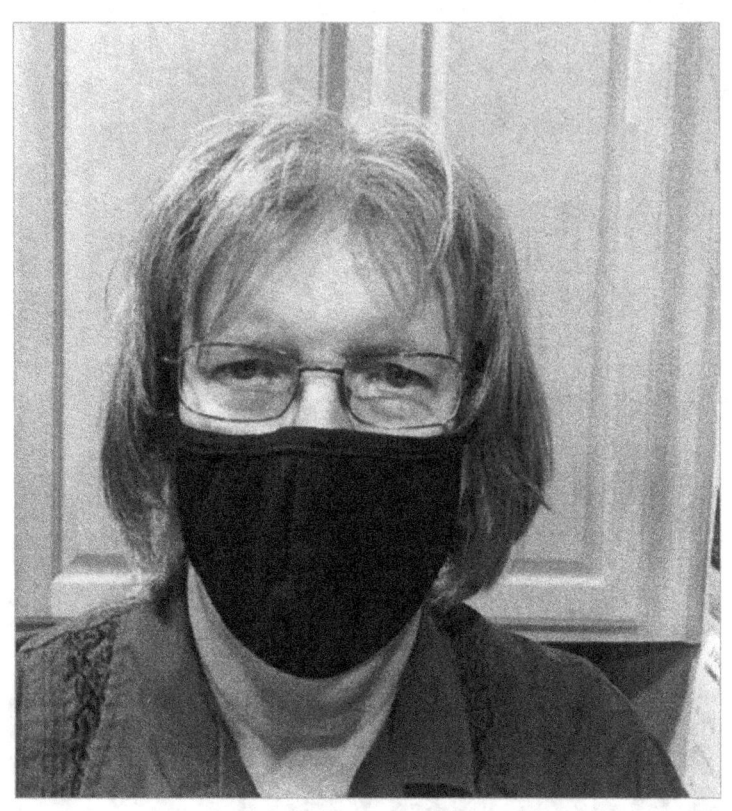

Ron fighting COVID-19 in 2021

Acknowledgments

Special thanks to the English cartoonist Ashleigh Brilliant (his real name) for permission to use some of his many Pot-Shots.

Thanks to all the people who edited various drafts of the manuscript including Michael Tolle, Bruce Frohman, and Alice Peck at Marvelous Editions. I probably should have accepted more of your suggestions.

Most of all, thanks to Judy for reading and rereading my hundreds of manuscripts over the last fifty years as well as for a million and one other things. As I always say, "Lucky me."

Want to Contact the Author?

If you'd like to contact Ron and tell him how much you like or dislike his book, or share some of your own experiences as an unknown writer please email him directly at Zentranshumanism@aol.com.

www.ingramcontent.com/pod-product-compliance
Lightning Source LLC
LaVergne TN
LVHW021700060526
838200LV00050B/2436